Staging Ancient Greek Plays

Staging Ancient Greek Plays
A Practical Guide

Michael Ewans

methuen | drama

LONDON · NEW YORK · OXFORD · NEW DELHI · SYDNEY

METHUEN DRAMA
Bloomsbury Publishing Plc
50 Bedford Square, London, WC1B 3DP, UK
1385 Broadway, New York, NY 10018, USA
29 Earlsfort Terrace, Dublin 2, Ireland

BLOOMSBURY, METHUEN DRAMA and the Methuen Drama logo
are trademarks of Bloomsbury Publishing Plc

First published in Great Britain 2023

Cover design: Ben Anslow
Cover image © Donald Cooper

A catalogue record for this book is available from the British Library.

A catalog record for this book is available from the Library of Congress.

ISBN: HB: 978-1-3503-8131-5
PB: 978-1-3503-8130-8
ePDF: 978-1-3503-8132-2
eBook: 978-1-3503-8133-9

Typeset by RefineCatch Limited, Bungay, Suffolk

To find out more about our authors and books visit www.bloomsbury.com
and sign up for our newsletters.

CONTENTS

PREFACE

This book seeks to convey to practitioners, students and teachers what I have learnt from my experience in twenty-six years of translating and directing nine full productions and countless workshops of Greek tragedy and comedy at my university (1983–2009), together with my further experience as the translator/director of professional productions of Theocritus' *Love Magic*, Euripides' *Medea* and Aristophanes' *Lysistrata* in proscenium arch theatres in 2019 to 2022. The translations have all been published, together with theatrical commentaries analysing the staging of each scene and ode.[1]

I write as a scholar-practitioner. I left the Department of Classics here for the Department of Drama, part-time in 1974 and full-time in 1982, since I was frustrated by not being able to explore the practical dimensions of Greek drama through directing productions and conducting workshops (also so that I could freely pursue my other research interest, modern opera). And I make no apology for the subjectivity of some parts of this book; I am intent on presenting to readers the results of my own experiences as a researcher, a translator and a director, as few people combine all three of these roles on a production. I believe that the insights that I have gained are valuable enough to share with other practitioners, teachers and drama students.

I dedicate *Staging Ancient Greek Plays* to the drama students at The University of Newcastle, Australia, who participated in

---

[1]See Ewans, M. entries in the Works Cited. I am grateful to Orion and to Oklahoma University Press for permission to reprint extracts from them in this book.

my first nine productions and my many workshops; to the two colleagues who added their professional experience, Barry O'Connor in the parts of Apollo (*Eumenides*) and Agamemnon, and Carl Caulfield in the lead role of Trygaios in *Peace*; to Claudia Bedford, who performed the extremely demanding title role in my professional production of *Medea* in 2021, as well as Lysistrata in 2022, and the other actors who worked alongside her in those productions. This book could not have been written without the creative work of all of them. But above all, I have to thank my long-distance collaborator at the University of Exeter, Emeritus Professor Graham Ley, who has worked in parallel with me since our pioneering joint article on the *orchēstra* as an acting area in 1985, contributed two translations and commentaries to my Everyman edition of Sophocles, and arranged for a memorable workshop with professional actors, which was convened by the two of us at Exeter in 2007 on scenes from my then unpublished translation of Aristophanes' *Acharnians*. He is the author of three important books on practical aspects of Greek drama (see Recommended Reading). Thanks are also due to the anonymous readers for Methuen Drama for helpful and constructive comments on the drafts, and especially to Anna Brewer for her continuous support as editor from first drafts to publication.

This book is designed to furnish practitioners who wish to stage or workshop Greek tragedies and comedies with the information that they need -- though non-practitioners who are interested in performance may also find it valuable. It is not intended for classical scholars. I hope that any such scholars who may read it will forgive me for giving abbreviated arguments and limited references on some issues that have been hotly debated among them, in some cases at considerable length.

The University of Newcastle, Australia

Michael.Ewans@newcastle.edu.au
ewansm7@gmail.com

NOTATION

Positions in the playing space are not notated by the modern system of upstage, downstage, etc. but by combinations of the following letters:

B   Back
C   Centre
E   Extreme
F   Front
L   Left
R   Right

So for example EBC denotes a position at the extreme back of the playing space, right in front of the central doors in the *skēnē* façade. EBL denotes a position next to the entrance (*eisodos*), on the left from the actor's point of view while CL denotes a position on the central cross-axis but to the (actor's) left of the centre spot, in-between C and ECL, which is a position on the left edge of the playing space on that same cross-axis. BC is halfway between the doors and the centre of the playing space, FC halfway from the centre to the extreme front centre (EFC).

DATES

All dates are BCE.

SPELLING

I have used Greek spellings rather than Roman (so Klytaimestra not Clytemnestra), with a few exceptions that include Aeschylus, Medea, Hecuba and *Bacchae*, rather than Aischylos, Mēdeia, Hekabē and *Bakchai*.

TRANSLATIONS

Except where otherwise stated, translations are by the author, reproduced with permission from the publishers of the books whose details are in the Works Cited as Ewans, M. 1995, 1996, 1999, 2000, 2010 and 2011. The excerpts from the *Oresteia* have been revised for a new edition currently in preparation.

Introduction: Adaptation and Interpretation

An *adaptation* of Greek tragedy or comedy takes place when an *auteur* or *Regietheater* director takes a translation of a Greek text, rewrites it (often very extensively, with new names and sometimes new characters) and presents the result in a staging that does not seek to replicate the dynamics of the original drama; the aim is usually to reconfigure the play so that it is relevant to some particular contemporary issue or concern. A controversial example was Peter Sellars' performance billed as a production of Aeschylus' *Persians*, staged in 1993 in response to the Gulf War of 1991 to 1992; the Persians became Iraqis expressing a vitriolic hatred of the USA. Apart from outraging patriotic members of the American audiences, this production inverted the fundamental concept of Aeschylus' original play, in which the Persians are the oppressors defeated by the courage of vastly inferior numbers of Greeks.[1] Bierl (2010) describes a number of 'postdramatic' performances in Europe that similarly should not have been billed as productions of Aeschylus' *Oresteia,* since they reshaped it drastically to stage a contemporary agenda. Recent times have seen extreme reimaginings, in which very little of

---

[1]Cf. Goldhill 2007: 133–4.

the original play is recognizable, such as Robert Icke's *Oresteia* (2015), in which the choros is eliminated, and Simon Stone's *Medea* (2020), a play 'after Euripides' in which the characters and much of the situation have been considerably altered. But relatively close adaptations under new titles, such as Luis Alfaro's *Electricidad* (2003), which relocated Sophocles' *Elektra* to a Latino slum in Los Angeles, or Seamus Heaney's *The Cure at Troy* (1990) 'after Sophocles' *Philoctetes*', play a very important role, since they both appeal to prospective audience members who may know nothing about Greek tragedy and comedy, and also invite discourse with those who do know the original plays on which they are based.

Adaptations have been widely discussed and are the subject of a substantial volume;[2] and there is no doubt that most of the writers and directors who refashion Ancient Greek drama, often reconfiguring their rewrites to inhabit a local contemporary setting in order to reflect their own preoccupations, do so in a sincere desire to give their productions relevance to their particular audience.

However, I advocate an alternative model that I call *interpretation*, where the resources of the modern stage are harnessed to presenting as far as possible the essence of what can be recovered of the original dramas by Aeschylus, Sophocles, Euripides and Aristophanes. Greek tragedy and comedy speak to us today precisely because the crises that they dramatized for their original Athenian audiences raise disturbing echoes for us in our twenty-first-century life. It would be overbold to claim that the issues they raise are 'universal human issues', but they dramatized situations that resonate in many contemporary societies, including, but very definitely not only those of, the English-speaking West. They do not need adaptation to make them relevant. And they can, if well performed, provoke both emotion and profound thought, since they are the work of master dramatists.

---

[2]Liapis and Sidoropoulou (eds.) (2021). Cf. esp. Meineck 2021: 77–90.

To interpret these plays onstage we should first do all we can to recover their meaning(s), and then work out which modern theatrical modes will best transmit those meanings to a contemporary audience. This calls for an understanding of how these plays work in the theatre, both ancient and modern, and for a number of approaches different from those that are helpful in performing modern drama (or even Shakespeare). Practitioners should be informed about the important features of Ancient Greek performance (Chapter 1), about some wider major issues, with which dramaturgs and directors will want to engage before staging these plays (Chapter 2) and about techniques through which their power can be conveyed to a modern audience (Chapter 3). The Appendix surveys performances available on YouTube and other AV resources, from the perspective that has been developed earlier in the book. A further Appendix is available online, containing synopses of all the extant plays, which may help you to choose a text for a workshop or full production.[3]

I do not seek to encourage a 'fidelity' that is unattainable, given the state of the evidence – and which is also undesirable – but to suggest ways of achieving historically *respectful* productions that release the power of the Ancient Greek plays to entertain, to elicit emotion and to provoke thought today. My observations are based upon productions staged before largely Caucasian audiences in an Australian post-industrial city; but I believe and hope that they have ramifications for all practitioners, regardless of the country, community and cultural climate in which they seek to perform Ancient Greek plays.

---

[3]https://www.bloomsburyonlineresources.com/staging-ancient-greek-plays

1

The Original Conditions of Performance[1]

1.1 The festivals of Dionysos

In Athens, tragedies, and later comedies, were performed at the festivals of Dionysos. Dionysos was 'first and foremost the god of wine and intoxication';[2] but he was also a god of fertility, and the god of *ekstasis* in general – of standing outside your normal self in an altered state, which could be created by wine, dancing and ritual. Dionysos, though terrifying if rejected and defied (see Euripides' *Bacchae*), had the power to augment the value of life through attainment of *ekstasis* by his worshippers; and most importantly for our purposes, this state could be achieved by the act of impersonation, the putting on of a costume and mask and assumption of a personality other than your own, which is the essence of the new medium – drama.

---

[1]This chapter covers only those aspects of Ancient Greek theatre that are essential for modern directors, drama teachers and actors to know and consider. For fuller accounts of the festivals and cultural context, of more interest to students of classical civilization, cf. Storey and Allan 2013, Chapter 1 and/or Raeburn 2016, Chapter 1.

[2]Heinrichs 2012: 62.

Tragic festival performances probably began in 501,[3] and the competition for comedy was added in 486.

The Great Festival of Dionysos was held in March, at the start of the sailing season, and thus attracted other Greek spectators to Athens as well as the domestic audience, which represented adult male citizens of all classes – farmers, city workers, intellectuals and aristocrats, together with resident foreigners – and women and children at the back of the theatre.[4] By the mid-fifth century it had become not only a religious celebration and a showcase for Athens' great invention, drama, but also an opportunity to proclaim the civic greatness of Athens through ceremonies that included an exhibition of the tribute paid that year by the city's subject allies, whose representatives were doubtless also present.[5] Three playwrights were selected to compete in the tragic competition, each presenting a group of three tragedies and a satyr play, and three to five playwrights competed for comedy, each presenting one play. The prize for tragedy was a goat, hence the name *tragōidia* ('a song at the goat-sacrifice').[6] The name 'comedy' comes from the Greek word *kōmōidia* ('a song of revelry'). The playwright was called a *didaskalos* ('teacher'); he was responsible not only for creating the script and composing the music, but also for teaching them to the actors and the *aulos*-player, choreographing the lyrics and directing

---

[3]Connor 1989.

[4]The presence of women has been contested, but the issue seems to me to be settled by Aristophanes *Peace* 960ff., a joke which is simply incomprehensible if they were not present and seated at some distance from the performance area. Cf. Olson 1998: 254–5 *ad loc.*, with references, and Henderson 1991. *Pace*, e.g. Storey and Allan 2013: 39.

[5]The political aspect of the festival was first emphasized by Goldhill 1990. But Green 1994: 8 rightly brought attention back to the religious and social dimensions, which are more important; and a balanced view has prevailed since then. Bassi (1998: 220–1) argued that the procession of *ephebes* (young men entering into adulthood, in military armour) countered the 'feminization' of the actors in the plays by the act of impersonation, especially of women and girls.

[6]Storey and Allan 2013: 75.

the production. He sometimes took one of the acting roles (though Sophocles abandoned acting, apparently because his voice was too small for the theatre). Early in his career, Aristophanes asked someone else to direct his comedies for him because of his lack of experience.

Each tragic playwright had to compose a satyr play to follow his presentation of three serious plays. They were sometimes linked loosely to one or more of the preceding tragedies – for example, Aeschylus' *Oresteia* was followed by *Proteus*, dramatizing an episode in Menelaos' return home from Troy. The choros was made up of satyrs, followers of Dionysos and avid would-be consumers of sex and wine – men in bearded masks, who were naked except for a furry loincloth with an erect phallus protruding at the front and a horse-like tail from the rear. One satyr-play survives complete – Euripides' *Cyclops*, dramatizing the famous episode from the *Odyssey* where the hero is trapped by, and conquers, a man-eating, one-eyed giant; and there is a substantial fragment of Sophocles' *Trackers*, together with smaller fragments by Aeschylus that support the claim in antiquity that he was a master of the satyr play.[7]

The actors were all male because of the relative seclusion of females in Athenian society, the need for freeborn women not to expose themselves by public performance and 'the received view that women are not what they seem'.[8] It is a fascinating paradox that some of the finest roles for women in the world theatre repertoire were created by male poets to be impersonated by male actors in an extremely patriarchal society. They must have been expert performers of the female, both with the voice and with the body (see further below **1.5** on costumes and masks); and specialists in female song and dance were undoubtedly cast in such roles as Kassandra (Aeschylus'

---

[7]*Cyclops* is available in several translations; Sophocles' *Trackers* in Ewans (ed.) 2000: 151–62, and with the ending reconstructed in Lancelyn Green 1957; Aeschylus fragments in Ewans (tr.) 1996: 117–22. Tony Harrison wrote a remarkable play inspired by the fragment of *Trackers*; Harrison 1991.
[8]Bassi 1998: 141.

Agamemnon and Euripides' *Trojan Women*) and Elektra (Aeschylus' *Libation Bearers* and Sophocles' and Euripides' *Elektra* plays). Froma Zeitlin (1990: 85) offers an explanation for the power of female roles in tragedy, which I believe to be substantially correct: 'by virtue of the conflicts generated by her social position, the woman is ambiguously defined between inside and outside, interior self and external identity; she is already more of a "character" than the man, who is far more limited as an actor to his public (social and political) roles'.[9]

Around 442, a formal competition for tragedy and comedy was also added to the winter festival of Dionysos, the Lenaia, held in January. A smaller number of plays were presented then. There were also local performances in the demes, the outlying districts of Attika.

1.2 Performance practice

The original performances of Greek tragedy and comedy were very different from any modern form of theatre. The dramas were performed in the Theatre of Dionysos, a vast open-air space, with an audience estimated at between 8,000 and 12,000 people.[10] The audience for tragedy watched three masked men doubling the solo individual parts and twelve (later fifteen) masked choros[11] actors playing a collective character; together they acted out in speech and song a new version of a 'myth' – an old, traditional story about heroes of

---

[9]Euripides' Medea is the most complex character in the surviving Greek plays; see Swift 2016 and on performing her role cf. Ewans 2022: 1–8.

[10]By the time Menander's comedies were performed in the late-fourth century, the theatre had been reconstructed and enlarged to hold approximately 17,000 people.

[11]I use the Greek spelling throughout to remind readers that the Greek *choros* was nothing like the chorus of a modern opera or musical.

the past (see **2.2**). These plays confronted their audiences with serious contemporary issues and with wider truths about human nature. Fifth-century comedy also engaged, very directly, with social and political issues; up to five actors and a choros of twenty-four performed either a burlesque of myth or a play set in contemporary Athens, but with many fantastic events.[12] In the fifth century, plays were performed only once; new plays were expected each year.[13] There was absolute freedom of speech, and the plays were distanced from the cut and thrust of everyday political debate in the assembly and legal debate in the courts. This distance was both physical, since the theatre was 1 kilometre away from the Pnyx where the Assembly was held and 1.5 kilometres from the Agora where much other public business took place, and temporal; holidays were set aside for the festivals. So the tragedies and comedies could raise 'the more unwieldly, problematic "big questions" of life in the *polis*'.[14]

The barriers to full understanding of Greek drama are substantial. We lack:

- Inside knowledge of the culture.
- A direct relationship with the stage shape and its techniques.

---

[12]Sometime in the mid-fourth century, the comic choros was reduced to fifteen, in alignment with that for tragedy. By this time, however, the choros no longer engaged in the action, but simply provided interludes between the five Acts into which plays had by then been divided.

[13]As a special tribute to Aeschylus after his death, it was decreed that anyone who sought to revive his tragedies could be 'granted a choros' – i.e. permitted to perform them. (The centrality of the choros in fifth-century drama is demonstrated by this formula.) And Aristophanes' *Frogs* was revived in the year after its premiere, because of its relevance to the critical situation in Athens (**3.5.3.2**). In the fourth century the rule was relaxed, and there were many revivals, mainly of Euripides.

[14]Wilson 2000: 67.

- Accurate copies of the original Greek texts, which have to be reconstructed from partially corrupt mediaeval manuscripts and fragmentary papyri.[15]
- The ability to translate these rich verse texts adequately.
- Knowledge of the choreography and music of the sung lyric sections.
- Original stage directions.
- In addition, very few dramas survive: six by Aeschylus (out of eighty known titles), seven by Sophocles (out of 120), eighteen by Euripides (out of ninety) and two by unknown authors, wrongly ascribed to Aeschylus (*Prometheus Bound*) and Euripides (*Rhesos*). As for comedy, complete plays by only one playwright, Aristophanes, survive from the fifth century; but we have eleven out of forty – just over a quarter of his output. No tragedy survives from the fourth or third centuries, but one comedy by Menander (*Dyskolos*, 'The Old Curmudgeon', 316) survives complete, together with substantial fragments of twelve others, one of which, *The Girl from Samos*, is sufficiently preserved to make a performance restoration possible.

Despite all this, the tragedies are so powerful and the comedies of Aristophanes so brilliant that their immediacy often makes them seem less dated than many far more modern plays. They have had an enormous legacy, since they were exported and performed throughout the Greek-speaking world in and after the fourth century, and were then widely imitated and studied in Rome; and they have been constantly translated, studied, responded to, performed and adapted ever since their rediscovery in the Renaissance.

---

[15]This work has been undertaken by skilled editors, and modern editions have restored all but the most corrupt passages in the Greek texts. There remain, however, many textual decisions that are contested, and translators sometimes need to make difficult choices.

1.3 The playing space

1.3.1 *Theatron* and *orchēstra*

This is the basic concept of Greek theatre, imitated by modern arena theatre designs. There was a steeply sloped *theatron* in which the audience was seated,[16] surrounding three sides of a rectangular or (less probably) circular *orchēstra* ('dance floor'), about twenty metres square or in diameter,

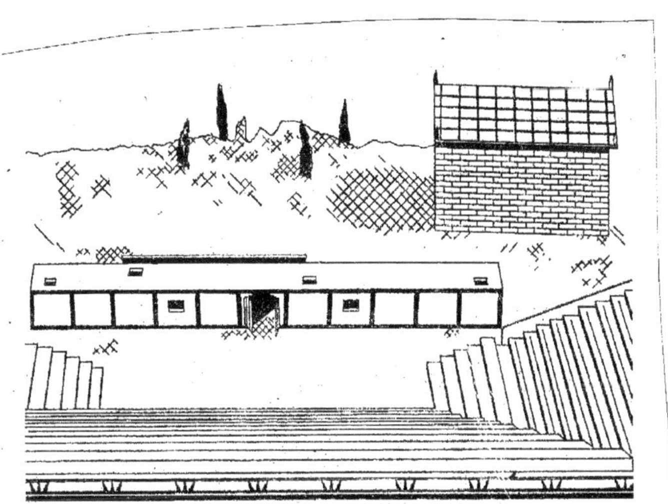

FIGURE 1: *The Theatre of Dionysos in the fifth century BCE, assuming a rectangular shape. Note the double doors in the centre of the skēnē, the windows and the access to the practicable roof. The mēchanē or crane is not shown, as its design is uncertain. © Michael Ewans.*

---

[16]The Greek name *theatron* means 'seeing place', emphasizing the visual element in drama as opposed to the Latin 'auditorium' meaning 'hearing place'.

which was the performance space.[17] Behind it, from 458 at the latest, was a long one-storey temporary wooden building, the *skēnē* (scene-building); see **1.3.2**.

The priests (the Priest of Dionysos in the central seat of honour), the Archons (government officials), the leaders of the tribes, the generals and leading politicians sat in the front rows on stone seats with backs; there were perhaps further stone seats for VIPs in the first few rows, including the Council of 500 and war orphans, who were specially honoured. Then there were wooden benches further up the hillside for the remainder of the audience. Note that both actors and audience could only enter and leave the *skēnē* and *theatron* before and after the performances by crossing over the playing space, in marked contrast to the separation of actor and audience entries in most modern theatres.

This was of course an open-air theatre, which brings with it the group dynamic of a mass audience who can see each other as well as the action in the playing space. The performances sometimes aroused intense emotions; one play by Phrynichos, *The Sack of Miletos,* was banned because it was too close to home, dealing as it did with a recent disaster to an Athenian ally.[18] W. B. Stanford in his classic study *Greek Tragedy and the Emotions* (1983) noted how the close proximity of the spectators to each other, the presence of Dionysos in the form of wine and

---

[17]The shape of the fifth-century *orchēstra* at Athens is contested, as the remains are slight and concealed under subsequent re-buildings. Some recent archaeologists, including Goette (2007) and Papastamati-von Mook (2015), have argued for a rectangular shape; but the long-held view that it was circular continues to be maintained by many scholars. However, Hughes 2011: 61 (cf. 59) notes that there is no circular *orchēstra* extant anywhere before the mid-fourth century (either the 'Lycurgan' reconstruction of the Theatre of Dionysos or the theatre at Epidaurus, whichever came first); but there are several examples of rectangular or trapezoidal theatres from the fifth century. Rehm (2002: 39–41) mounts a convincing opposition to the circular theory, with full bibliography. What matters, however, is that regardless of the shape, the audience surrounded the action on three sides.

[18]Tragedies based on history rather than heroic myth were extremely rare; there is only one other known example, Aeschylus' extant play *Persians*.

the fact that they could all see each other, led to a dynamic akin to that of a modern football crowd; and he remarks that, given the amount of passion expressed by the characters in tragedy (which he documents), the Ancient Greek audience was likely to have been far more emotional than a modern Northern European, North American or Australasian indoor audience.

By sitting at or near ground level, the VIPs got the worst view of the action – but, of course, they were there as much to be seen as to see the performances (the royal boxes in large eighteenth- and nineteenth-century theatres, placed right beside the proscenium arch with atrocious sightlines to the stage, served a similar purpose). Everyone else had a downward perspective, their eyes drawn down into the *orchēstra*. The *skēnē* acted as a sounding board, and the acoustics were very good; so both the words and music and the patterns of movement in the plays were very important.[19] The principal visual focus was on the centre point; there was probably a small altar there for the preliminary religious rituals, but it was removable either to make the dominant centre point available for actors, or for central props, e.g. the tombs in the first half of Aeschylus' *Libation Bearers* and in Euripides' *Helen*. In Greek tragedy the spectators looked down on a group of humans in their sufferings, trapped inside the playing space, just as the gods looked down on *them* from the temples on the Acropolis behind the *theatron*.

The focus in Greek drama is on outdoor, public space. Reflecting actual contemporary conditions in the city, indoor life was viewed only in its consequences for public life. Hence the importance in many plays of the *skēnē* threshold between the inner world of a house or palace, and the outer, normally male-dominated world of public affairs.[20]

---

[19]A tragic actor, Hegelochos, ruined his reputation simply by mis-pitching a vowel and transforming Euripides *Orestes* 279, 'after the storm I see a calm again' into 'after the storm I see a weasel again'. The audience burst into laughter; cf. Aristophanes *Frogs* 304–6 with Dover 1993: 231.

[20]Cf. especially Aeschylus' *Agamemnon*, where Klytaimestra dominates the threshold, controlling who shall enter the palace, and how – until she is baulked by Kassandra's refusal to enter at her command.

The mass of people congregating for the festival was dwarfed by the landscape. From the upper seats in the *theatron* there was a view to the port of Piraeus 10 km away; and the Acropolis soared up behind the theatre.

1.3.2 The *skēnē*

The first three surviving plays of Aeschylus do not seem to need a scenic background, but they do need a place for actors to change costumes and masks – perhaps just a tent (*skēnē* literally means 'tent').[21] By the time of Aeschylus' *Oresteia*, 458, there clearly is a long, low wooden building behind the *orchēstra*, temporarily erected for each festival. It was known as the *skēnē*, and it had a flat roof, an entrance through one central pair of doors,[22] and at least one window so sounds from inside could be heard. It could be used to represent a house, palace, temple, cave, grove, tent, etc. *Skēnographia* (scene-painting) panels were placed each side of the doors, using the new art of perspective painting to represent these locations for an individual play or, where a scene-change occurred, for part of a play.[23]

---

[21]Cf. Ewans 1996a: 169–70.

[22]The theory that there were two or three doorways into and out of the *skēnē* in the fifth century was refuted by Dale (1969: 118–19 and 126–7; cf. Taplin 1977: 344 and 349–50); her findings are confirmed by my successful stagings with one set of double doors of both tragedy and comedy (which might seem to present more difficulties). The three-door theory has been revived by Raeburn ((2016: 65) in relation to the same scene that Dale discusses, Aeschylus *Libation Bearers* 870–91; but she had convincingly refuted him in advance. However, two doors (and two windows) are probably required in Aristophanes' *Assemblywomen* (392?); and by the time of Menander's comedies in the late-fourth century, three doorways, representing entry into separate houses, were required; they were probably installed at the time of the 'Lycurgan' reconstruction in the mid-fourth century, to accommodate the requirements of Middle and New Comedy.

[23]On *skēnographia* cf. Ley 1989 or more briefly Ley 2006: 23–4.

There was no raised stage in front of the *skēnē*; the *skēnē* doors opened directly onto the *orchēstra*, in which solo and choros actors interacted. Several scholars have assumed that there must have been a stage for the solo actors, failing to appreciate the degree of interaction between solo actors playing individuals and the choros playing a collective character that these dramas, created in a democracy, need in performance. There is no archaeological evidence for a stage, and for arguments against it see Pickard 1893 (decisive, but ignored), and more recently Ley and Ewans 1985.[24] Sir Peter Hall's notorious 1981 production of Aeschylus' *Oresteia* at the National Theatre of Great Britain showed by constructing one, the impracticability of a raised stage creating two separate playing areas. And my practical experimentation, workshopping scenes with and without a raised stage, has shown that it renders many important scenes unplayable, or at least playable only with considerable artifice. For an example of how interactive scenes between a solo actor and a choros can work in an *orchēstra*, see 1.7.

1.4 Staging conventions

There were three entrances and exits. Two were *eisodoi*, passages leading onto the playing space at the sides of the *skēnē*; by convention actor left entry was normally from the city near where the action is set, while actor right entry symbolized arrival from the countryside, other cities or the seashore. The *skēnē*'s set of double doors at the front centre of the building opened onto the extreme back centre of the *orchēstra*. These represented exit into or entry from whatever location the drama had established the *skēnē* as representing. Sudden entry was only possible through the *skēnē* doors;

---

[24]Cf. also Ewans 1995: xx–xxii (with bibliography), Wiles 1997 chapter 2 esp. 33, and Ley 2006: ix ff. *Contra* Goldhill 2007: 8 and Raeburn 2016: 4. Dunbar and Harrop (2018: 154) are clearly unfamiliar with the relevant research.

actors arriving by either *eisodos* came into view of an increasing number of the spectators on the opposite side as they approached the playing space. They therefore had to be in character as soon as they drew within sight, but not in action until they entered the *orchēstra*.

The *ekkuklēma* ('rolling out machine', a platform on wheels) was used to bring out an interior scene that would otherwise be invisible in the shadows inside the doors. Its use is virtually certain for the climax of Aeschylus' *Agamemnon* (458), where Klytaimestra is displayed, covered with blood and sword in hand, over the bodies of her victims Agamemnon and Kassandra, and the parallel scene in the sequel, *Libation Bearers*. The convention was that actors could, when desired, step off the tableau to interact more closely with the choros and other characters already in the *orchēstra*; the character then becomes as if outside, after beginning as if inside but disclosed and visible to those outside (this is less complex in practice than it sounds!). The *ekkuklēma* was a vital means of bringing before the Greek spectator at climaxes the indoor world, which was otherwise debarred from their sight; if it were not used, tragic events that have happened inside could only be narrated by a messenger from within – which happens, e.g. in Sophocles' *Oidipous the King* (1223ff.). In my 1987 open-air production of Sophocles' *Aias*, we used an *ekkuklēma* to wheel Aias out from his tent, naked to the waist and covered in blood, slumped among the corpses of cattle, sheep and a sheepdog. To my surprise and delight, the Newcastle audiences accepted this Ancient Greek convention completely.[25]

The flat roof of the *skēnē* was practicable. Notable examples of its use are to be found at the very start of *Agamemnon*, where the Watchman on the roof of the palace begins the play; and in Euripides' *Orestes*, where in a thrilling finale Orestes

---

[25]I prefer to use the Greek spelling rather than the Latin *Ajax* because at one point (430ff.) the hero realizes how his name reflects the Greek cry of grief, 'Aiai!'. Also to remove the play from any thoughts of domestic cleaning products!

and Pylades, having (they think) murdered Helen, hold her daughter Hermione hostage on the roof and threaten to kill her if her father Menelaos persists in his attempt to force open the *skēnē* doors below them. The roof may also have been used for some appearances of gods, e.g. the colloquy between Athena and Poseidon at the start of Euripides' *Trojan Women*; perhaps ghosts – Dareios in Aeschylus' *Persians* and Polydoros in Euripides' *Hecuba* – might also have played their scenes from there.

A later innovation was the *mēchanē*, which was first used in a surviving play in Euripides' *Medea,* 431. It was a crane with its base behind the *skēnē*, a counterweight, and a flying platform capable of carrying one or two actors.[26] It was used at the climax of some tragedies, usually to fly a god or gods in to above the *orchēstra* to resolve the issues between the human characters, and often to found a cult. For good examples cf. Euripides' *Ion, Elektra, Iphigeneia among the Taurians, Helen* and *Orestes*. The Latin phrase 'deus ex machina' is derived from the *mēchanē*. Aristophanes uses it for comic effect in *Peace* and *Clouds*, and parodies its use in Euripides' *Andromeda* in *The Women's Festival* 1009ff. (cf. **3.4.2.1**).

There were no programmes in the Greek theatre (many of the audience would have been illiterate), so there was a convention of entrance announcements. It was evidently an unwritten rule that on arrival, new characters would be named, either by somebody already in the *orchēstra*, or by their own announcement – always within eleven lines of arrival. And when they arrive, they will speak. (Aeschylus deliberately violated this rule with Kassandra in *Agamemnon,* leaving her ignored for 169 lines after her entry, not actually named for a further eighty-three and only bursting – sensationally, after this build-up – into highly agitated song yet another thirty-nine lines later; cf. **3.5.2.3**.)

---

[26]For an illustration of a reconstructed model cf. Hughes 2011: 53.

1.5 Costumes and masks

Costume was contemporary; no attempt was made to reproduce the costumes of the heroic age in which the tragedies were set.[27] The solo actors in tragedy wore long, intricately patterned robes appropriate to the heroes and heroines whose parts they were taking; choros members wore costume appropriate to the character they were playing, as, for example, in a vase that illustrates two choros members preparing to play female maenads.[28] The one who has his mask on is fully in character (and looks very realistically female as he tries out a dance step); the other, who is adjusting his costume and does not have his mask on, is not yet in character. The actor became the character not when he got into costume, but at the moment when he put on his mask.[29] Tragic actors wore a soft boot, the *kothurnos*; comic actors wore the leather boot of the everyday Athenian. In comedy, actors wore a body-stocking with leggings and sleeves; it had painted-on nipples, a belly button and pubic hair for scenes of stage nudity. Over it most actors playing male roles wore a very short *chiton*, a tunic which only went down to the upper thigh. They also wore a long, dangling, leather phallus that protruded below it, and fake testicles.[30] They often wore a short cloak over the *chiton*. Female characters wore a *chiton* that descended to their ankles, on occasion covered by a long cloak.[31] Almost all comic actors had padded rumps, bellies, false breasts when playing female characters and (from around 415) padded chests, adding to the distorted effect created by their masks; in the 'Choregoi

---

[27]Rehm 2017: 76.

[28]Boston, Museum of Fine Art.

[29]This vase is discussed in Wyles 2011: 63 and Wiles 2007: 25–6.

[30]Cf. the vase paintings and terracotta figures illustrated in Compton-Engle 2015 or Hughes 2011, and Aristophanes *Clouds* 537–9. In *Lysistrata*, as the women's sex strike takes its toll, men who enter later in the play sport *erect* phalluses.

[31]Compton-Engle 2015: 17ff.

vase'[32] a character from tragedy named Aigisthos wears tragic dress, full-length and richly embroidered, while actors playing a comic choros wear the short *chiton* and phallus of comic costume. In the many lost comedies, which were parodies of myth or of actual tragedies, it is likely that the heroic characters who were being sent up wore the same type of costumes as their counterparts in tragedy, as does Aigisthos in this scene from *Demes*.

Solo actors and choros members wore large *prosōpa*, which we misleadingly translate as 'masks', since their purpose was not to conceal but to *reveal*. The word *prosōpon* means 'face', and these larger than life-size complete head coverings were worn to increase visibility and enable the most distant spectators, up to 100 metres away from the playing space, to identify the gender and age of the character being played from the colour and length of their hair. This was normally black for all except the old, whose hair was grey (there are however some blonde characters in tragedy, e.g. Euripides' Iphigenia and Helen). Female characters had long hair except when in mourning, and males were differentiated between bearded adults and unbearded youths.[33] Tragic masks were idealized but realistic;[34] most, but not all, comic masks were distorted, with beards for the males, gaping mouths, snub noses and a distorted facial expression for both genders – but actors playing attractive young women, such as the Servant who comes out to tempt Xanthias/'Herakles' into Persephone's palace at *Frogs*

---

[32]In the Museo Archeologico Nazionale di Napoli. Illustrated on the cover of Wyles 2011.

[33]It is possible that some tragic masks did more than simply indicate gender and age, if the Lipari terracottas reflect fifth-century practice; see Wiles 2007: 64–5.

[34]Wyles 2011: 8–9 and Hughes 2011: 167 use the term 'naturalistic', which I would prefer to avoid because of its close association with a particular type of theatre developed in the late-nineteenth century. For images of tragic masks cf. either Wyles 2011 or Wiles 2007. Comic as well as tragic costumes and masks are illustrated in Green and Handley 1995; and specifically for comedy cf. Hughes 2011 and Compton-Engle 2015.

503ff., wore realistic masks and did not have distorting body padding.[35] Named contemporary individuals appeared in several of Aristophanes' comedies, Lamachos the bellicose general, Agathon and Euripides the tragic playwrights, Socrates the philosopher and Kleon the demagogue politician and general among them. Doubtless they were portrayed in masks that displayed a caricatured version of their actual features.[36]

The mask was a key feature of Greek dramatic performance; it enabled male actors to play characters of both genders and all ages. But there is more. As David Wiles writes, 'the power of the tragic mask lay in the transition that it effected, from the world of Athens to the world of myth'.[37] And: 'Athenian audiences experienced a voice in the theatre as the voice of the mask activated by the actor, and not the voice of the actor mediated by the mask.'[38] In comedy, rather than assuming the character portrayed by the mask, the actor presented it (Hughes 2011: 171).[39]

It might be objected that a mask cannot realistically display the emotions of a character such as Medea, who in the course of her play plumbs the depths of despair, the heights of vengeance and many emotions in between – all of which the modern unmasked actress can and must express with her face as well as her body. But the display of emotion was not the function of the mask: 'the whole body of the actor had to be engaged in finding the impulse which creates a fusion of sound and meaning'.[40] If you have worked even with the modern,

---

[35]Cf. Compton-Engle 2015: 36, and the scene portrayed on a vase at Green and Handley 1995: 57.

[36]Aristophanes makes fun of this in *Knights* (230ff.), where just before the appearance of Paphlagon (the Kleon figure) he has one of the characters say: 'And don't be scared – it won't look just like him;/ because they are afraid, none of the mask-makers would make/a close likeness. But he will still be recognized; the audience are no fools.'

[37]Wiles 2007: 66.

[38]Wiles 2007: 170.

[39]On character cf. further **2.2**.

[40]Wiles 2007: 150.

neutral mask, let alone as I have done with replica Greek masks, you will have become aware that spectators inscribe emotion onto the mask, in accordance with the text delivered by the actor and the postures and gestures that he or she adopts in performance.

I believe that the main reason why the Athenians capped the maximum number of solo speaking actors at three in tragedy and five in comedy, was clarity and audibility. It is difficult to be certain who is speaking, in an open space, from behind masks (since the source of the voice is not visible), with all-male actors. Hence there is careful signalling in the text to indicate who is speaking in the few places in tragedy where more than three people (three soloists together with members of the choros) are in interaction; cf. e.g. Sophocles *Oidipous the King* 631ff.

1.6 Actors

Thespis, the legendary inventor of tragedy, had one actor (himself) interacting with the choros, and presumably changing masks and costumes during the choral odes to portray different characters. Aeschylus increased the number to two before his earliest extant play, *Persians* (472); and either the young Sophocles or Aeschylus again in later life (sources differ) added a third actor in or before the year of Aeschylus' *Oresteia* (458). These actors played all the parts of individual speaking characters in tragedy, though mute 'silent faces' (i.e. extras) were always allowed. Actors playing both men and women wore free-flowing costumes and low, soft boots, so plenty of movement was possible.[41]

---

[41]It was a long-held belief that they wore high buskins, like Roman tragic actors, which would have made rapid movement impossible. But a glance at the vase paintings, e.g. in Green and Handley 1995, is sufficient to refute this view.

The actors doubled parts as a play unfolded, and some doublings are fascinating; the great but flawed king Agamemnon and subsequently the inferior usurping tyrant Aigisthos in Aeschylus' *Agamemnon*; the unwittingly murderous wife Deianeira in Sophocles' *Women of Trachis* and then her heroic husband Herakles, who is reduced to effeminate status by the agony he suffers, trapped in the poisonous robe that she gave to him. An actor could look for modes of expression, both verbal and physical, which indicated the similarities, as well as the differences, between related individuals whom he played consecutively.[42]

1.7 The choros

The choros is the most difficult aspect of Greek drama for us to appreciate. On proscenium arch stages, it is often shoved off to one side; and there has been a general assumption that the members of the choros were static between their dances (which some people call 'interludes'), with one spokesperson when they are speaking to solo characters. I believe that all of this is completely wrong. The problem is heavily compounded by our ignorance of the choreography and the music. But we must endeavour to understand the choros; it was central to the dramas, and indeed choroses were central to Greek life. Competitions for mass male choral songs (dithyrambs) also featured at the Festival of Dionysos, along with those for tragedy and comedy, and dithyrambs were performed at other festivals. Meanwhile, Pindar, Bacchylides and other lyric poets were commissioned by those who won at the Olympian, Pythian, Nemean and Isthmian Games to compose victory odes for choroses to sing and dance on their return home. And Laura Swift (2010) has demonstrated that tragic Choroses incorporate or refer to genres of song that were customary occurrences in

---

[42]On acting for the modern stage, see **2.2** and **3.4**.

Greek everyday life; the *paean*, the *epineikion* (victory ode), the *partheneion* (choros sung by unmarried girls), the *hymenaion* or wedding-song and the *thrēnos* or ritual lament.

A fundamental mistake has been made in Greek texts and in most translations by labelling the choros' contributions to dialogue and song as CHORUS. Certainly, they *are* a choros – but they *play* a collective character, in both tragedy and comedy. So they should be given that character's name in the text: Elders in *Agamemnon*, Furies in *Eumenides*, Councillors in *Antigone* and Sailors in *Aias*; Women of Corinth in *Medea*, Bacchae (female worshippers of Dionysos) in *Bacchae*, Old Men and Old Women in *Lysistrata*, where Aristophanes divides his choros of twenty-four in two to reflect the gender conflict at the heart of the comedy (**3.5.3.1**), Birds in *Birds* (twenty-four different identifiable varieties!), etc.

They are witnesses and participants. In Greek tragedy the sufferings of heroes are not seen in Hamlet-like isolation with monologues on an otherwise empty stage. The problems of individuals are seen as part of the troubles of the *oikos* (household) – and even more as part of the problems of the *polis*, the city-state. In Aeschylus' *Agamemnon*, the Elders of Argos, played by the choros, have a principal role (and more lines than any one of the solo characters); by this choice civic focus is given to everything that is done. Klytaimestra's murder of Agamemnon is presented in the final scene not only as a moral outrage but as political, the death of the rightful king leading to usurpation by the tyrant Aigisthos. And in the sequel *Libation Bearers,* a group of mere captive, foreign, female household slaves proves to be the most powerful and influential choros in all of the surviving tragedies, guiding Elektra and Orestes on their quest for revenge and luring Aigisthos to his death. It is true that although choros characters sometimes threaten to take drastic action, e.g. storming the doors of a palace or house when a murder is taking place inside (*Agamemnon* 1350ff., Euripides *Medea* 1275ff.), they actually don't. But in two surviving tragedies of Aeschylus, the choros is the main character (*Suppliants* and *Eumenides*). And in several comedies of Aristophanes, the choros character is quite prominent – e.g. *Acharnians, Peace* and *Lysistrata.*

The choros provides stability and continuity in the plays; they are the only actors who stay in one role throughout (the solo actors change masks and costumes during choral odes to play different characters); and the time-span of the play is in the choros' keeping.[43] The convention was that a choral ode may cover the elapsing of as much, or as little, real time as the playwright wishes – only a few minutes or hours in most cases, but up to three weeks during the second Choros in *Agamemnon,* and enough days for a journey on foot from Athens to Sparta and back in *Lysistrata* Choros 5. The choros contributed the lyric and dance dimension, a sung and choreographed enactment of issues. Although we often listen to piped music between scenes, the Athenians filled the 'intervals' with a rich vein of lyric commentary, often introducing extra, mythical dimensions. The odes are frequently reflective – but performed in character, and usually intensely engaged with the action of the surrounding scenes, though sometimes providing an oblique contrast (cf. e.g. Euripides *Elektra* Choros 2, 432ff.). Often a Choros will take flight from the situation at the end of the preceding scene, and end with material that foreshadows or overshadows the action of the next scene (cf. e.g. *Agamemnon* Choroses 2 and 3). Alternatively, in a Choros the choros character can react to what has just happened with what the spectators may feel to be inappropriate joy, which is dispelled in the following scene. This device was specially used by Sophocles (e.g. *Antigone* Choros 6 and *Oidipous the King* Choros 4, both placed right before the revelation of disaster).

---

[43]There are an extra choros of Argive soldiers at the end of Aeschylus' *Suppliants,* a choros of Athenian women and girls who escort the Furies, now become the Solemn Goddesses, to their new home at the end of his *Eumenides,* and an extra choros of Huntsmen at the start of Euripides' *Hippolytos,* who reappear later in the play to engage in a lyric interchange with the main choros of Women of Troizen (1104ff.). So supplementary choroi were permitted if the sponsor (*chorēgos*) was able to afford them.

Dance and song, and the use of myths, lift the drama onto a more emotional and universal plane than spoken words. This alternation of lyric and spoken verse was fundamental to Greek tragedy and comedy.[44] Solo actors could also sing, and therefore dance, when their character was in a highly emotional state, e.g. Xerxes in the finale of *Persians*, Kassandra in *Agamemnon* (**3.5.2.3**) and Elektra in the title role of Sophocles' tragedy (**3.5.2.2**) and of Euripides' (e.g. 112ff.); and solo singing was used increasingly as the fifth century progressed.

It has been the scholarly orthodoxy that during scenes there was one spokesperson interacting with the solo characters on behalf of all, and that the choros remained relatively static; these beliefs, for which there is no extant evidence, have influenced many productions (cf. some of those discussed in the Appendix). I would challenge both suppositions. In our productions in a replica of the original playing space, individualizing of choros person movements, and distribution of lines between different choros members, have been highly successful; indeed, necessary to avoid monotony. Why assume that the Greeks liked monotony? Wilson (2000: 353) rightly remarks that: 'The basis in ancient sources for the modern editorial practice is virtually non-existent. Even the habit of assigning the lines of spoken dialogue to an individual leader rather than the whole group rests on no more than an assumption about the collective's need for a "spokesman".'[45] This assumption is anachronistic; a lack of division of dialogue between all the members is very unlikely in a democratic *polis*

---

[44]Every Aristophanic fifth-century comedy contains at least one *parabasis*, an extended section in which the choros steps out of the play – but not out of character – to address the audience on matters of current concern, often speaking and singing on behalf of the poet himself. Cf. **3.5.3.2**.

[45]The idea of a spokesperson is a (very) frequent modern misunderstanding of the meaning of the Greek word *koruphaios*, which actually means the man who initiates choral movement by giving a cue to the *parastatai*, the next in line; Aristotle *Politics* 1277a 11–12. After Agamemnon's death-cry at *Agamemnon* 1343ff., it is obvious that the dialogue *must* have been divided between the twelve individual Elders, so why not elsewhere?

where every citizen participated in the Assembly. So in my translations, choral contributions to dialogue are prefixed with, e.g. '1 ELDER', with the expectation that directors and actors will agree on which member of the choros will speak a line or lines. And a static choros makes little sense when blocking in an *orchēstra*. Possibilities for choral movement during scenes to express their shifting relationship with solo characters are endless; I provide an example later in this section.

In Greek drama, the solo character is almost constantly seen in his or her interrelationship with members of a community. Solo monologues after the opening speech of a play are therefore very rare, since they require the choros to leave the playing space, which is normally only done during a change of scene.[46] Aias' solitary suicide speech in the middle of Sophocles' tragedy (815ff.) attracts great attention precisely because of its uniqueness in the surviving plays.

The Greek theatre has its own unwritten rules about the relative power relationships of positions in the *orchēstra*; and power relationships are often central to scenes in both tragedy and comedy, as you quickly discover in rehearsal using a playing space surrounded on three sides. Entry from the *skēnē* at EBC (extreme back centre; for this notation system cf. p. x) pulls focus backwards from the natural point of

---

[46]Euripides *Helen* 386–514 is an exception; the scene does not change while the Greek Women go into the palace and return. There are changes of scene in Aeschylus' *Libation Bearers* (cf. Ewans 1995: 174–5) and *Eumenides,* and Sophocles' *Aias*; each change involves exit by the choros, setting or striking a prop in the centre of the *orchēstra* while they are absent and changing the *skēnographia* panels before the choros' re-entry in the new location. Fifth-century comedy was more flexible, cf. e.g. Aristophanes *Acharnians* 1–622 and *Frogs* 1–320, where there are three changes of scene in each play before the *skēnē* settles down to represent Dikaiopolis' house and Plouton's palace respectively. In both plays it is likely that panels depicting a house were preset and used throughout the comedy (cf. also *Peace*). However, in *Birds* two sets of panels are necessary; a woodland setting up until the first *parabasis*, and after that, when the scene has changed to Cloudcuckooland, clouds in the sky.

most power, which is C; advancing via BC to C consolidates the power of the entering character. However, movement further forward, into the front half of the playing space, reduces a character's power, since the mask's face can be seen by less and less of the audience until at EFC only those directly ahead of the actor can see it.

It is not essential that the face of every *prosōpon* be always visible to the majority of the audience, though movement that enables much of the audience to see the front of the mask is desirable, and indeed the arena playing space positively invites movement, in contrast with a box set in the end-on proscenium arch theatre. So a confrontation between two characters of equal strength could well begin with them standing at BR and BL, while a confrontation in which the characters are not of equal strength would be effective if one character is at BR and the other, weaker character is at FL (or BL and FR). Note that in all three of these configurations, the face of at least one of the characters is fully visible to most of the audience, and that is sufficient for them to engage with the action.

Here is an example of how a substantial amount of movement by a solo actor and a choros can generate an effective staging of a scene in the *orchēstra*. This is a short example of how power relationships can be conveyed by blocking; an interaction between solo actor and choros that I have staged in a full production and refined in subsequent workshops, in a replica of the Greek theatre shape.

Aeschylus, Eumenides Scene 2

Klytaimestra's Furies are occupying the orchēstra, *and the* skēnē *represents the temple of Apollo at Delphi.*

Enter **Apollo** *from the* skēnē, *armed with a golden bow and arrows.*

Apollo 1 Get out, I tell you, leave my house at once:
you must be gone from this prophetic shrine   180
or you will feel a gleaming arrow's bite

winged on its way by my bow's golden cord.
The pain will make you spit black foam
and puke up all the clotted human gore you've
      quaffed.

2 It is not fit that you draw near these halls;   185
your home's the slaughterhouse where heads
      are lopped,
eyes are gouged out for vengeance, boys' young
      manhood is destroyed
by cutting off their testicles; where men are
      mutilated, stoned
to death, and groan with piteous cries
impaled on stakes. Do you not realize   190
it is because you love such hideous feasts
that all the gods spit you away? The way you look
tells the whole story; creatures such as you
should live inside the lairs of lions that feast
      on blood,
rather than grind pollution into soil as pure as this.   195
3 Get out, you flock without a shepherd; there's
      no god
who would delight in herding you.
1 Fury   4 Lord Apollo, listen to us in return;
      you are yourself not just a part-conspirator in these
      events;
in every way your actions show you are their cause.   200
Apollo   How? You may speak long enough to tell
      me that.
1 Fury   Did you not give an oracle that he should
      kill his mother?
Apollo   That he should punish those who killed his
      father; what of that?
1 Fury   You then stood ready to receive him with
      the blood fresh on his hands?
Apollo   I did, and told him he must come here as a
      suppliant.   205

1 Fury   And now you slander us because we
        follow him?
Apollo   Yes, you're not fit to enter such a shrine.
1 Fury   But this has been ordained; it is our task.
Apollo   Oh, really? Let me hear it; boast about your
        splendid privilege.
1 Fury   It is our duty to pursue a matricide from house
        and home.   210
Apollo   Well, what about a woman who has killed her
        husband?
1 Fury   She would not have killed a true blood
        relative.
Apollo   5 Then you reduce to nothing and despise
     the sacred vows of marriage, sanctified by Zeus
     and Hera the fulfiller; you dishonour and
        reject Cypris,   215
     the goddess who gives humankind their closest
        bond.
     The bed, where man and woman are united by their
        destiny –
     Justice defends that even more than sacred oaths.
     6 And so if you are less than strict in your pursuit of
        murderers,
     and don't exact a penalty or visit them with all
        your anger, then   220
     I say you have no right to persecute this man;
     for now I find that some misdeeds enrage you, while
     on others it is obvious you take a softer line.
     7 The goddess Pallas will watch over how this case
        comes out.
1 Fury   8 I will not ever let him go.   225
Apollo   Well then, pursue him. Give yourself more toil.
1 Fury   Don't try to cut my privileges down by words.
Apollo   I wouldn't want to have your privileges.
1 Fury   No; whatever happens you are held in
        high regard beside the throne of Zeus.
     But I – since I am driven on by mother-blood –   230

will go in search of justice. **9** I will hunt Orestes to
the end!

Exeunt, right.

Apollo **10** And I will give protection, and will save
my suppliant;
the anger of a man who turned to me for refuge
would be terrible,
among both men and gods, if I could help, and failed.

Exit into the skēnē.

When Apollo emerges from his temple to confront the Furies,
armed with a golden bow and arrows, they have just been
addressing him in his absence ('I hate Apollo, and he will not
help that man escape', 173). To do this they would most
naturally be facing towards the *skēnē*, spaced out in a straight
line ECL-C-ECR (or perhaps in a slight curve backwards,
with the choros members in the middle of the line a little nearer
to FC).[47] Apollo can then storm forward to BC to confront
them (**1**), and since the whole audience can see his face there is
no problem with the Furies' having recently turned their backs
on the majority of the audience. He abuses the Furies vigorously
in his opening speech, perhaps moving along part of the line to
address different individual Furies as he threatens them with
his bow and an arrow (179–84). He then draws back slightly
to begin 185ff. (**2**), but he cannot maintain the calm that
persuasion requires; his anger increases as he resorts to
emotional rhetoric (190ff.), and (**3**) he might well threaten the
Furies again with his bow on the very aggressive lines 196–7.

A dialogue follows (**4**; 198ff.), in which Apollo finds himself
on the back foot, metaphorically, because of the logic of the
Furies' arguments and their calm and dignified approach; this

---

[47]The choros is most powerful when spread out to dominate part or all of the
playing space, weaker when bunched together. Cf. Ley 2014: 58.

can be symbolized in the blocking if individual Furies advance when they speak a metre or so towards him from their places in the line, and if the dialogue is distributed so that Furies from different sides of the centre alternate their contributions. This forces Apollo both to retreat towards the temple and to turn from side to side to answer the Furies' questions and statements. His position of relative power (BC) has been weakened by the movement of individual opposing Furies towards him from across the central part of the playing space, and by the allocation of their lines.

Apollo breaks off the dialogue (5: 213ff.) and bursts out into a display of emotional rhetoric; his weakness at this point is very effectively symbolized if he breaks through the line of Furies into the weaker front segment of the *orchēstra*. They would then turn as one to face him, their masks now visible to the centre block of the audience for the first time in this scene and displaying their hostility through their posture. But (6) Apollo recovers himself in 219ff., and so should regain the rear half of the playing space to deliver the rest of the speech. This indicates his return to some degree of power, and he can finish (7) with a disdainful turn away from them on 224.

The Furies are not persuaded; they express their determination to pursue Orestes (8). Three individual Furies exchange words with Apollo, and as they do so the whole choros should move to form a compact group near the mouth of the right *eisodos*, and (9) face Apollo for the last six words of 231, perhaps delivered in unison. Then they exeunt, bent over in a hunting posture to follow Orestes' trail 'since I am driven on by mother-blood' (230).

Apollo has recovered his own determination, despite a verbal encounter that he has not won (this foreshadows his sophistic arguments at the trial in Athens later in the play). His three lines after the Furies have left (10) should be delivered from BC, before he turns and exits back into his temple. The encounter leaves Aeschylus' audience puzzled – and curious about what is to come; the radiant, young, male sun-god, son of Zeus, is ill-tempered and has little justification for what he says, while the Furies, hideous, old, female creatures from the everlasting darkness below the earth, are calm and rational. The blocking proposed above reinforces this central aspect of the scene.

This is just one example of how the shape of the Greek theatre stimulates quite sophisticated patterns of movement to illuminate the shifting relationships between characters. I could furnish many more from my eight full productions and many workshops of scenes from both tragedy and comedy created in a replica of the Greek theatre shape. And it is worth noting that as I gained greater confidence in using the shape through experience, the amount of movement in my productions increased. Ancient Greek drama was very much physical as well as textual.

1.8 'Realistic' or 'stylized'?

Some scholars assume without argument that Greek tragedy must have been a stylized form of theatre. For example, Katherine Worth did this as she tried to argue that there is an an affinity between the theatre art of Samuel Beckett, e.g. in *Play* and *Happy Days*, and Greek tragedy. And more recently David Raeburn referred to the recognition scene in *Libation Bearers* as 'this highly stylized form of drama'.[48] But the Greeks did not have a vocabulary for contrasting 'realistic' and 'stylized' theatre – that only comes to the fore in the early- to mid-twentieth century, when the Naturalistic style inherited from the late-nineteenth century European theatre came to be contrasted with the formalist and stylized drama of Expressionism.

If the Greeks had had the ability to make this distinction, I believe that they would have claimed that their theatre is

---

[48]Worth 2004: 264 and 281; Raeburn 2016: 60, cf.68 on the trial scene in *Eumenides*.

realistic.[49] Ritual almost by definition consists of repeating sacred rites identically; but new, different dramas were required each year at the festivals. And they naturally on occasion dramatize acts of ritual, such as making offerings to a god or deceased hero, since these were parts of normal Greek life; but that does not make the plays themselves ritualistic, nor stylized. We have seen that masks and costumes were realistic. And the tragedies dramatized the sufferings of characters from myth, of people who were believed to have actually existed in the heroic age, and the actions of gods in whom the vast majority of the audience believed (**2.2–3**). Despite what Raeburn says about the recognition scene in *Libation Bearers* (which when properly acted in a realistic style can be profoundly moving),[50] he himself believes there was 'naturalness' in the acting,[51] and that although post-Stanislavskian method acting is wholly inappropriate, we see 'real people acting recognizably in recognizable human situations'[52] – with details of characterization (only) when appropriate (cf. **2.2**). Furthermore, Worth's belief that Samuel Beckett's plays, in which characters are encased to the neck in large jars (*Play*) or buried first to the waist and then after the interval to the neck in a mound (*Happy Days*), have any affinity with Greek tragedy is quite misguided. I believe that in Greek drama solo characters and choros used vigorous movement to illuminate the text that they performed. As Graham Ley has rightly written: 'the cliché that Greek tragedy is static is laughable, almost as ridiculous as the belief that it is classically serene and composed: it is frantic, urgent

---

[49]This was argued as long ago as Vickers 1973: 53–4 and Walcot 1976: 67. Arnott (1989: 10) correctly insisted that the steeply sloped arena theatre shape is an intimate one; it is a false assumption that a large *theatron* and *prosōpa* automatically imply a remote, distant actor-audience relationship.

[50]Cf. my production on YouTube Aeschylus *Libation Bearers* (1983 production) 13:02–18:13.

[51]He rightly contrasts this with the sign language of Japanese classical theatre.

[52]Raeburn 2016: 6. Cf. Dunbar and Harrop 2018: 53–78 against applying Stanislavsky's method to Greek tragedy.

and explosive.'[53] Greek tragedy is only 'unrealistic' if it is compared to the spoken prose plays of Chekhov, of Ibsen's middle period and of the 1950s British 'kitchen sink' dramas of Osborne, Wesker and others. But theirs is a very different kind of realism.

---

[53]Ley 2014: 24.

2

Values, Myth and the Individual, the Gods and *Moira*

This chapter presents a discussion on some larger issues that practitioners should find useful, before we address the more detailed aspects of form, meaning and staging in Chapter Three.

2.1 Greek and modern values

There are major differences between Ancient Greek and modern Western values, and anyone embarking on a production should be aware of them. In Ancient Greek society, the excellence of a man was to have the status of an *agathos* (literally a 'good man'); this was achieved by gaining *timē* (loosely translatable as 'honor', but measured very practically in terms of material possessions and power). Birth, wealth and military ability were the three criteria for excellence. The fundamental duty of the *agathos* was to help his *philoi* ('friends') and harm his enemies – both help and harm being equally important. His *philoi* were the family members living in his own *oikos* (household) – his wife and children, and elderly parents – and his other relatives and close friends. In order of priority the a*gathos* himself came first, followed by his family and then by the *polis* or city-state of which he was a citizen. Other people did not count at all.

There was no word corresponding to 'guilt' – an internalized emotion; the motivating force for all *agathoi* was to avoid an action that was *aischron* – shameful, humiliating in the eyes of others. Intentions did not matter; results were all. The word *dikē*, which we translate as 'justice', was much closer to the concept of an eye-for-eye revenge than to the more humane parameters of 'justice' in modern Western societies. In the Athenian democracy, only adult citizen males had a voice in the assembly and the law-courts; all females were under the tutelage of their *kyrios* – their father, then their husband or if they had neither living their other nearest male relative. The ideal excellence of a woman was *sōphrosynē* – modest, prudent conduct, with a heavy emphasis on chastity.[1]

Naturally, this value-system, of which the two paragraphs above are the briefest of outlines, came under attack. In the increasingly monetized society of the sixth and fifth centuries, landed aristocrats who regarded themselves as the sole *agathoi* found that men whom they could previously disdain as *kakoi* ('bad men', the opposite of *agathoi*) by reason of their ignoble birth, claimed equality with them on the basis of the wealth (i.e., *timē*) they had amassed, usually through commerce. This led to a rise in Athens in the mid- to late-fifth century of demagogues such as Kleon, who could address the Assembly persuasively, and had gained enough *timē* by his business operations to rise to political power. (Aristophanes, himself an aristocratic *agathos*, mercilessly pillories Kleon as a 'leather-seller' in *Knights* and other plays.) Furthermore, the fundamental belief that all human beings are responsible for

---

[1]On Greek values the definitive work is by Adkins (1960 and, more accessible to those who are not classical scholars, 1972). Though there has been some debate generated by his work, the main conclusions have not been seriously contested.

their actions, regardless of whether a god or a *daimōn* (a godlike power such as Persuasion, Ruin, or Desire; see **2.3**) had influenced them, began to be questioned in the late-fifth century by the sophists. One of them, Gorgias, wrote a defence of Helen, whose adulterous elopement with Paris caused the Trojan War; and in Euripides' *Trojan Women* (914ff.), Helen herself argues that she was not responsible for the disaster because of the influence on her of Aphrodite, a goddess who has power even over Zeus himself (she is roundly rebutted by Hecuba). And whereas in *Oidipous the King* (c. 425), Oidipous accepts absolute responsibility for killing his father and marrying his mother, in Sophocles' last play, *Oidipous at Kolonos* (407/6), Oidipous argues that his ignorance of what he was doing makes him free of blame (977 and ff.).

This is the environment in which tragic and comic poets pictured the behavior of men and women. Some heroes act in ways, or have dilemmas, to which we can readily relate; at the climax of Aeschylus' *Libation Bearers* Orestes, sword in hand and facing Klytaimestra who has bared the breast that suckled him, turns to his close friend and asks: 'Pylades, what shall I do? Should I not fear to kill my mother?' (899). Antigone's determination to bury her brother Polyneikes is also easily understandable. Less so perhaps is Sophocles' Aias; furious that the armour of Achilleus was awarded to Odysseus rather than to himself, he plots to murder all the other Greek chieftains – but is deluded by the goddess Athena, who makes him slaughter sheep and cattle instead. When he recovers from his madness, he is ashamed, not because of his plan to murder his royal enemies, but because he failed to accomplish the massacre successfully (364ff.); he broods on how Odysseus will now be able to laugh at him. Critics and audiences are divided to this day about Euripides' Medea; her husband Jason dumps her to marry a young princess, and instead of accepting the divorce calmly as a *sōphrōn* woman should (Jason, 1369), she adopts male values, explicitly referencing the code of helping friends and harming enemies (797, 807ff.); she contrives the deaths both of the princess-bride and of her father the king, who has threatened Medea with exile. This is startling enough; but Medea goes further. The only way in which she can kill her enemies implicates her two young sons; and rather than leave the boys alive for the relatives of the royal family to take revenge, she kills them herself and then escapes on a flying chariot provided by her grandfather the Sun-God. Like Aias, she is motivated by a determination not to be shamed by being laughed at by her enemies (404, 797, 1355).[2]

Only sometimes do co-operative virtues shine through; and even those are often tinged with self-interest. Towards the end of *Aias,* Odysseus argues against Agamemnon that he should allow even this man who planned to murder them both a decent burial ('his greatness means more to me than our enmity', 1357):

Agamemnon   So you are telling me to let them bury him?
Odysseus   I do; one day, I'll need a burial myself.
Agamemnon   It's all the same; everyone works just for
    himself.
Odysseus   And whom should I more rightly work for
    than myself?

(1364ff.)

There are several scenes in comedy that remind us that the Ancient Greek value code is very far from Christian ideals. When Dikaiopolis in *Acharnians* has concluded his private treaty with the Spartans, a suffering farmer who has lost both his oxen in the war begs him for just a little Peace to rub into his infected eyes. Dikaiopolis refuses him outright: 'I'm sorry, but I'm not a public service doctor' (1030). And several of Aristophanes' characters relish the disappointment of enemies – for example, the Farmers in *Peace* eagerly anticipate the sufferings of a gourmet, Melanthios, when he comes to market

---

[2]On Medea and Greek values see further Ewans 2022: 1–6.

and finds that the greatest delicacy, Kopaic eels, has sold out (1009ff.; 'All those who see him will rejoice!').

One of the tasks of the modern director and cast is to enable their audiences to take an imaginative leap into a world whose values are very different from those preached by Jesus, and not to judge the actions of characters in Ancient Greek drama by inappropriate criteria. A realist might well say that this is not too difficult; there are many examples of politicians today who practise values similar to those of the Ancient Greeks – placing themselves first, their relatives and political party next, the good of the country third (if at all) and doing harm to their enemies whenever they get an opportunity. In the West, women are no longer under the control of a *kyrios*, but since the 1800s their path towards recognition of equality and positions of authority has been shamefully obstructed by many males, who have felt threatened with the diminution of their own power. Only in recent years has it become widely recognized in some advanced societies that women have the right not to be submissive. (In theatre, film and television, highly talented female directors, scriptwriters and playwrights are at last being given the opportunities that they deserve. And male playwrights and scriptwriters are also creating female characters of all ages who possess greater power and agency.)

Although we have established courts with a considerably more humane concept of justice than that exhibited in many Greek tragedies, they have by no means eliminated violent acts of revenge from contemporary society; atrocities both great and small are common even in those countries that regard themselves as part of the developed world and have sophisticated judicial systems relatively free from corruption. Accordingly, it is possible to establish connections across the divide of values, which bring out the relevance of these plays to contemporary audiences. It is essential to achieve a performance style that encourages the audience to empathize strongly with the characters and their situations, and for this reason I believe that it is effective to develop productions that are fundamentally realistic and costumed in modern dress.

Audiences must experience the performance as akin to a situation that could happen today.[3] Chapter 3 will explore techniques that should enable this feeling to be induced.

2.2 Myth and the individual

Sophocles' *Women of Trachis* begins with this monologue by a middle-aged but still beautiful woman:

> There is an old saying that runs like this:
> You cannot be sure that someone has had
> a good or a bad life until he is dead.
> Well, for my part, even with Haides not yet in sight,
>   I am
> certain that my life has been grim, a life to cry about.
> While I was still at home in Pleuron, in the house   5
> of my father Oineus, I faced the direst
> prospect ever faced by a bride in Aitolia.
> A river was my suitor, the river Acheloos that is,
> who came to ask my father for my hand in three
>   shapes;   10
> appearing, as you looked, as a sleek bull, or then
> as a glistening snake in coils, or again as a bull-head
> on a man's body, while streams of living water
> poured down through the bush of his beard.
> That's the kind of suitor I had to tolerate.   15
> Poor thing, I wanted to die, prayed and prayed that I
> would before I was put into bed with something like that.
>
> A great deal later, and to my delight
> Herakles came, the famous son of Alkmene and of Zeus.
> He launched himself into battle with this creature,
>   and in the contest   20

---

[3]As was stated in audience feedback for my productions of Theocritus' monologue *Love Magic* (2019: search YouTube Theocritus Love Magic) and Euripides' *Medea* (YouTube Euripides Medea Newcastle Australia 2021).

became my deliverer. I am not the one to give a blow
by blow account, because I wouldn't know how. Who
    could?
Whoever sat apart unmoved by what he saw then.
As for me – I sat there terrified, paralyzed by fear
that my beauty would in some way bring me to grief.   25
But Zeus, who presides over contests, gave us a happy
    result,
if this is happiness. I have my bed with Herakles, as his
    chosen bride;
but in it I breed fear on fear, always something new,
worrying on his account. Night after night takes up
the new load of worry and puts off the old, in
    succession.   30
Yes, we have had children together. But he has been
rather like a farmer who must take his plough to a
    distant field,
with one visit for sowing, and one again at harvest time.
His life has been just like that, back home and out,
constantly in service to someone or other, man that
    he is.   35

And now, when he is nearly at the end of his labors,
I feel these fears all the more sharply than before.
He killed the lord Iphitos, and since that time
we have lived here in Trachis, uprooted, in the house
of a close friend. Where Herakles has gone no one   40
knows. But he has left behind him, for me,
pain born of sorrow at his continuing absence.
I can almost feel sure that something has happened
    to him.
I'm not talking about a short space of time;
nearly fifteen months, and not a word about him.   45
Something dreadful has happened. That is the meaning
of the tablet he left behind with me, and I have often
prayed to the gods that it should not spell disaster.[4]

---

[4]Translated by Graham Ley in Ewans (ed.) 1999: 87–8.

The first question that a modern actress and director should address is the purpose that this speech serves as the opening of the play. One problem is that most of the original Athenian audience clearly had a good knowledge of myths – the stories of the gods and heroes – and of previous poetic versions of them. The playwrights took advantage of this;[5] but most members of a contemporary audience do not have such knowledge.

The first five lines are ominous as the opening of a tragedy; it was proverbial that you should 'count no man happy until he is dead', so the Greek audience would apprehend that the speaker is naïve and may well experience further sufferings as the play unfolds – as indeed she does, ending in her suicide. The next few lines establish her identity, without naming her; they would immediately recognize that she is Deianeira, second wife of Herakles, who had slaughtered his first wife and all their children in a fit of madness inflicted by the goddess Hera.[6] This tragic past might have provided Athenian spectators with an undertow to the plot of this new play, though it is never alluded to in *Women of Trachis*.

Deianeira laments Herakles' infrequent visits home because of his labours, and states how her fears have grown as he nears the end of them (36). She then concludes by referring to a tablet that he had left behind with her; it will play an important role after its contents are revealed in the second scene.

This narrative set before its original audience all that they needed to know before the action proper begins. But does it have anything corresponding to the 'subtext' that actors and directors explore in more modern plays? What are Deianeira's 'true feelings'? Is she, for example, pining for her absent

---

[5] Cf. e.g. the opening of *Agamemnon*, where Aeschylus foreshadows his striking variant on the Homeric version, in which Agamemnon was killed on his return home by Aigisthos, not Klytaimestra (*Odyssey* I. 28ff.); the Watchman refers to Klytaimestra as 'the waiting, hopeful woman who plans like a man' (11), and this theme is developed in the first half of the play.
[6] Euripides dramatized that myth in *Herakles*.

husband? Is she racked with sexual jealousy? Or is she anxiously fearing her husband's return, worried by the aggression of this notorious sexual predator and sadly anticipating further examples of the callous disregard with which he treats their children?

Such questions have no place in the interpretation of an Ancient Greek play. Deianeira tells us repeatedly that she worries about her absent husband – but her feelings are not clarified further, certainly not to a point where she can be held to be pining for him. Nor is she wracked with sexual jealousy – that will happen to her later in the play, when she is confronted with Herakles' new mistress Iole, and learns that he has sacked the city of Oichalia to abduct her. It is important not to believe that those developments are anticipated here in Scene 1. Finally, there is no evidence that she is fearful of her husband's return; on the contrary, later in this scene she sends her son Hyllos off to find his father, and in the next scene, which is her first interaction with the young women of Trachis played by the choros, she describes what is on the cryptic tablet, and asks: 'Am I to remain/ alone, lose the best man on earth?' (176–7).

The writing on that tablet is central to the development of the play. Herakles revealed its content to Deianeira on his last visit home; it contains a prophecy from Zeus' oracle at Dodona that:

> ... when he had been
> away a year and three months, out of the country,
> it was determined that at that time he would die,
> or if he managed to survive that particular term,
> he would live free from pain for the rest of his days.[7]

Now is the time when this oracle will be fulfilled, and Deianeira is in a state of terror because of it (175–6). The majority of the Athenian audience would know that the oracle was indeed

---

[7] 164–8 trans. Ley in Ewans (ed.) 1999: 92.

fulfilled in most versions of the myth by Herakles' death; they were watching for a new exploration in Sophocles' play of *how* that happened.[8] Deianeira, like all the speaking and singing individuals and choroses in Greek tragedy and comedy, is simply a mask, whose words and actions the actor presented to his audience; she has no existence beyond and behind those words.[9] As David Wiles has written: 'The mask belonged naturally to a theatre where selfhood was a function of exterior relationships, and there was no question of the audience peering to see what was going on inside [an individual's] mind.'[10] But *through* those words Deianeira has a living presence in a tense and frightening situation, which – despite her opening five lines – only gets worse for her and for Herakles as the play unfolds.

In Ancient Greek tragedy there are no rounded 'characters' in the modern sense of the word – people with individual mannerisms, internal psychology and particular character traits. Instead, most people live entirely for their aims in the situation confronting them in the drama; and in tragedy some of the most powerful characters (many but not all of them female) – including Aeschylus' Suppliants, Klytaimestra and Kassandra, Sophocles' Antigone, Elektra and Aias, Euripides' Medea, Hecuba (in two different plays), Herakles and Helen

---

[8]In most versions of the Herakles story, the gods raised him after his death to immortality and gave him the goddess Hēbē (Youth) as his bride. The absence of that happy ending, and Hyllos' condemnation of Zeus for his treatment of his son in the final lines (1264ff.), are notoriously grim aspects of *Women of Trachis*, an unpleasant surprise at the end of the play. Compare the absence of Klytaimestra's Furies at the end of Sophocles' *Elektra*. *Contra* Holt 1989, who thinks that the apotheosis is implied; but in Greek poetry (epic and lyric as well as tragedy), if an event from the 'standard' version of a myth is omitted, that is a deliberate and significant choice.

[9]In saying that the actor 'presents' an individual, I am not aligning Greek tragedy with Brecht's 'presentational' theatre and his concept of *Verfremdung* (distancing). Greek tragedy was designed to involve the audience deeply in the sufferings and emotions of the people who are represented in it. Cf. **1.3.1**.

[10]Wiles 2007: 271. Cf. **2.1** above on Greek values for the ways in which selfhood was 'a function of exterior relationships'.

– exist almost entirely in their emotions, using logical argument and reasoning in dialogue sections simply to gain their desires or justify their beliefs.[11] In comedy also, the principal characters have an overriding aim, and set out firmly to pursue it (e.g. Dikaiopolis in *Acharnians*, Trygaios in *Peace* and Lysistrata – all three in search of peace). The characters' words are the expression of their true feelings; there is no subtext, just a rich and complex tapestry of open and transparent poetic communication. People say what they mean and mean what they say (except of course when speaking ironically, and in scenes of deception).

It is the task of the modern actor to work out how to deliver those words, and act the part of the individual whom he or she is impersonating, as it is presented in each moment of the text of the play; not to explore behind the words, seeking to penetrate the psyche for thoughts and feelings that are not expressed overtly in them. This is a central truth that actors and directors must accept and work with, even if it goes against their training.[12] The company should be made aware of the background in myth to the play that they will be performing, and programmes will help the modern audience if they outline the events before the action; for example, with my 2021 *Medea*, a substantial section of the programme note described the back story, starting with the voyage of the ship Argo to Colchis, and going through to the situation when the play begins, since the Nurse's opening monologue takes some knowledge of previous events for granted.

---

[11]For example, in the dialogue between the Suppliants and Pelasgos at Aeschylus *Suppliants* 325–489, the *agōn* between Elektra and Klytaimestra at Sophocles *Elektra* 515ff., or that between Medea and Jason at Euripides *Medea* 446ff. For the reasons why many of the most powerful roles in Greek tragedy were female cf. **1.1**.

[12]Cf. Dunbar and Harrop 2018: 53–78 against trying to apply post-Stanislavskian method acting to Greek tragedy. Workshops and exercises that might help the modern actor to adapt to performing Greek tragedy can be found in Ley 2014, and Dunbar and Harrop 2018.

2.3 The gods and *daimones*

As Greek polytheism is a vast topic, the focus in what follows is on what practitioners should know; the roles that gods and *daimones* played in influencing human affairs in tragedy and comedy, and how we can respond to them in a modern production.[13] It will be seen that each of the three great tragedians had a very different viewpoint from the others; and that Aristophanic comedy treats almost all the gods, as it treats human beings, with complete irreverence.

2.3.1 Aeschylus

For Aeschylus, the gods and *daimones* are an immanent presence, interacting with and reacting to the actions of human beings. In his first surviving drama, *Persians* (472), Aeschylus dramatized the defeat of Xerxes' overwhelming invading forces eight years earlier by the vastly outnumbered Greeks – the Athenians at sea at Salamis and the Spartans on land at Plataia. In the world of the play, excessive wealth and prosperity may invite the jealousy of the gods, and those who go beyond their natural limits will be struck down. (But note that in *Persians* as in *Agamemnon* (459ff., 750ff.), it is not wealth in itself but wealth *accompanied by crime* that brings men low.) The ghost of the former king of Persia, Dareios, proclaims the depth of his son's folly:

> Ah! Too swiftly have the oracles come true, and Zeus
> hurled down fulfilment of the prophecies upon my son.
>   I'd hoped
> and prayed the gods would not fulfil them until after a
>   long time;

---

[13]2.3 and 2.4 are not burdened, as they could have been, with a large scholarly bibliography. I have preferred to focus on what we can learn from the plays themselves.

but when a man hastens along, the god joins in as well –
and now it seems a well of sufferings is pouring out
    for all our family.
My son, not understanding, in young folly brought
    them to
accomplishment; he hoped to yoke the sacred Hellespont
    as if it were
a slave, and bind its flowing stream, gods' holy Bosporos,
    in chains,
trying to make the ocean dance his tune; he cast leg-irons
over the stream, and made a mighty crossing for his
    mighty force.
It was not wise, since he is human, to suppose that he
    could overcome
all of the gods, especially Poseidon. Was this not mental
    disease
that overcame my child?

(739ff.)

By building a bridge across the Hellespont, Xerxes offended the sea-god Poseidon; and by attempting to conquer a European race, the Greeks, he recklessly exceeded his own Persians' natural sphere of influence, Asia (modern Asia Minor and the Levant); cf. 93ff., 181ff. and 821ff. So, Xerxes brought down upon himself an ominous prophecy of Persian arrogance and subsequent disaster that might otherwise not have been fulfilled for several more generations of kings: 'but when a man hastens along, the god joins in as well' (742). Furthermore, his troops in Greece desecrated the altars and shrines of the gods (809ff.) – just as the Greek troops did after the sack of Troy in *Agamemnon* (see below), incurring a similar disaster.

The *Oresteia* (458) begins with the Elders' narrative of a portent; as the expedition to Troy set out, two eagles devoured a pregnant hare and her young, and the seer Kalchas interpreted this as meaning that the goddess Artemis is angry with Agamemnon and Menelaos because of the loss of life of innocents that will occur when they attack and destroy Troy. He also foresees – though in obscure words – the avenging wrath of Klytaimestra to come (*Agamemnon* 105–59). Then onshore winds delay the departure of the expedition, and Kalchas receives a further insight – that the furiously angry goddess demands the sacrifice of Agamemnon's daughter Iphigenia before she will let the fleet sail (197ff.). And Agamemnon has a choice that is no choice ('He put upon himself the harness of necessity', 218); he must accept her justified demand.[14]

This narrative is the foundation on which the *Oresteia* rests, since the sacrifice of Iphigenia motivates the revenge-murder of Agamemnon by his wife on his return from the Trojan War (1412ff.). It portrays a world in which the gods react to human actions and enforce their consequences. Not too much later in *Agamemnon*, a similar pattern is seen; we learn that the victorious Greeks plundered the shrines of the gods in Troy and destroyed their altars. They, in return, suffered a great 'storm of anger from the gods' during their voyage home; it wrecked many of their ships and scattered the few that survived (see 338ff., 526ff. and 638ff.). Gods play a very important role in the remainder of the trilogy, as when Apollo's oracle tells Orestes that he must avenge his father or suffer torments both on earth and in the afterlife (*Libation Bearers* 269ff.); then that same god appears in person in *Eumenides* to defend him against pursuit by Klytaimestra's Furies, whom Aeschylus represented by the choros, violating an unspoken taboo in tragedy against exhibiting gods from the underworld, and doing so in a spectacular fashion.[15] And the

---

[14]It is Artemis' demand, not that of his fellow chieftains as in many commentaries and translations; Ewans 1975: 26–7 on line 214, endorsed by Winnington-Ingram 1983: 85. Cf. the translation in Ewans 1995: 8: 'her demand, her utter and insensate rage/for sacrifice of virgin blood/to stop the winds/is right. May all be well.'

[15]Legend has it that boys in the audience fainted and young women gave birth when the twelve Furies entered one by one from the *skēnē* (Ancient *Life of Aeschylus* 9 and Pollux 4. 110). We do not have to believe this story, but the very fact that it could be told shows the great impact of Aeschylus' *coup de théâtre* in *Eumenides*.

whole bloodstained saga of the trilogy is resolved by the calm, mediating influence of the goddess Athena, who also appears in person in the final play.

Daimones are godlike powers that we would call personifications (and so we should capitalize their names in translations, though naturally audiences are not aware of this); among them Fear, Destruction, Terror, Madness, Persuasion, Desire, Strife, Violence and Ruin. Every *daimōn,* like the gods themselves, can lead a human being astray from the course that his or her rational mind is attempting to pursue, and so cause tragedy. They are frequently invoked in Aeschylus, less so in Sophocles and Euripides.

2.3.2 Sophocles

Aias is probably Sophocles' first surviving play, but it cannot be dated more closely than between 450 and 430. (I am inclined to a date towards the middle of that period.) The probable date of *Antigone* is 438,[16] so twenty years after the *Oresteia,* which was Aeschylus' last set of plays. It is evident from these two tragedies that Sophocles' conception of the role of the gods in human life is very different from that of Aeschylus. With one exception, gods do not appear on stage in his seven surviving dramas, though the demigod Herakles appears on the *mēchanē* to resolve the issues at the end of *Philoktetes.* Sophocles' gods rarely react to human actions; the exception is Athena in *Aias,* ruthless in her anger at Aias' slighting of her assistance in battle (757ff.). She appears in Scene 1, and exhibits to Odysseus the maddened Aias, who has slaughtered cows, sheep and sheepdogs in place of the Greek kings on whom he sought revenge, but is still deluded that he has triumphed over his enemies. Her appearance is designed to make Odysseus, and the audience, aware of the dangers of excessive pride, in an almost Aeschylean speech that does,

---

[16]Lewis 1988.

however, at the end strike a new note, the possibility of *sudden, drastic* mutability in human life:

> **Athena**   Now you have seen this, you must never speak
>   a word of arrogance against the gods,
>   and do not swell with pride because you're greater
>   than another in your strength of hand or depth of
>   wealth.
>   One day can weigh down everything a human being is
>   and has
>   or lift it up again; the gods love prudent men
>   and hate those who are not.
>
> (127ff.)

In *Aias, Antigone, Women of Trachis* and *Oidipous the King* there is indeed sudden, unexpected and disastrous change in the course of just one day.[17]

In Sophocles there is none of the feeling of an integrated nexus of human actions and divine responses that is evident in the *Oresteia* – and highly probable in the Theban trilogy of 467, in view of the contents of the third play, *Seven against Thebes*, which survives. Instead, the gods are normally remote, issuing prophecies that are often in the form of if-clauses; *if* Aias leaves his tent during this one day of Athena's anger, he will die; if not, he will be safe (748ff.); *if* Laios has a son, that son will kill him and marry his own mother (*Oidipous the King* 711ff.). The choice is entirely up to the human being, though once he or she performs the dangerous action, the consequences are inexorable. Sophoclean gods do protest at human outrage, as when at the outset of *Oidipous the King* they inflict a plague on the city of Thebes to indicate their

---

[17]The Oxford English don John Jones formulated the concept of Sophoclean mutability in his pioneering book *On Aristotle and Greek Tragedy* (1962: 166ff.).

displeasure that it still harbours the murderer or murderers of Laios; or when Kreon in *Antigone* refuses to allow the burial of Polyneikes, and condemns Antigone to death for performing it; the prophet Teiresias takes the omens, and discovers extreme signs of *miasma* and divine disapproval. Kreon is only reluctantly persuaded by his Councillors to heed Teiresias' advice; but when he does, he reverses the order that the Councillors recommended (1100–1). He chooses to bury Polyneikes first, before going to free Antigone from the cave in which she has been immured; this decision brings about the deaths of Antigone, his son Haimon who was in love with her and his own wife Eurydike who is devastated by learning of these events and commits suicide. Again, the gods merely warn that what Antigone has called 'the unwritten/and everlasting laws made by the gods' (445–6) have been violated by Kreon's refusal to allow the burial of a corpse; the disastrous ending of the play is entirely the result of human actions – specifically those of Kreon, because of his stubborn inflexibility in the face of his son's pleas and Teiresias' reading of the omens.

In Sophocles' reinflection of the Elektra story, Apollo simply tells Orestes *how* to avenge his father – through deceit (*Elektra* 32ff.); the moral issues surrounding matricide and revenge-justice, which predominated in Aeschylus' *Libation Bearers* and *Eumenides*, are left entirely up to the human beings, and the two ruthlessly amoral avengers, Orestes and Elektra, do not make a favourable impression.[18] In *Women of Trachis*, the prophecy about Herakles, discussed above in **2.2**, is recognized by Herakles himself, when it has come true and he is dying in agony, as a sick joke played by the gods. He says that the Selloi,

---

[18]Against the long-held view that in Sophocles' play Orestes and Elektra are admirable heroic avengers cf. Kells 1973: 1–12 and Ewans (ed.) 2000: xxvii–xxxv. Finglass (2007: 8–10) discerns elements of both readings, and some sympathy for Elektra in the early scenes, but concedes that a negative view of the siblings dominates towards the end of the play.

who interpret the sounds of the great oak tree at Zeus' oracle in Dodona:

> told me that in this living
> and present time now I should obtain release
> from my imposed labors. I hoped for good success.
> But the meaning was only that I should die:
> there is no further labor for the dead.[19]

Sophocles' middle-period dramas present a singularly bleak world view.[20] The dramatist pictures life as in constant flux, and humans as being extremely limited in their power and their knowledge. The immanent gods of Aeschylus' integrated universe are no longer present, with their assurance that *dikē* will ultimately prevail, and the gods intervene in Sophocles only when a human action has offended against one of a few fundamental taboos. This was a time when rationalist, 'enlightened' thought at Athens was particularly severe in its attacks on both oracles and prophets. Apparently, Sophocles expected his audiences to find consolation in the reassurance that in his dramas prophecies turn out to be true, so there is some limited pattern in the universe, even if the consequences seem, from a human point of view, to be monstrously disproportionate (Herakles) or totally unjustified (Oidipous).

2.3.3 Euripides

Euripides' surviving dramas present different perspectives on the gods. On the one hand there are two plays, *Hippolytos* (428) and *Bacchae* (406), in which Aphrodite and Dionysos appear and give awesome displays of their power, inflicting destruction on men who have refused to accept their divinity;

---

[19]1169ff., trans. Ley in Ewans (ed.) 1999: 122.
[20]We lack any plays by Sophocles created before he was at least forty-five. The extant middle-period dramas are *Aias, Antigone, Women of Trachis* and *Oidipous the King*.

by contrast, in the majority of his plays human agency proceeds unimpeded through almost all of the action, usually in unexpected directions, with plots full of twists and turns – and a divine intervention on the *mēchanē* is sometimes needed to restore the 'normal' version of the myth; cf. e.g. *Iphigenia among the Taurians* and *Helen,* and above all *Orestes* (see below **2.4**). These fluctuations reflect the moral and intellectual turbulence of the late-fifth century, when belief in the gods was questioned, and new forms of tragedy, with a different kind of action, emerged to respond to the new realities (see **2.4**). The most remarkable feature of this period is Euripides' composition in the last year of his life of *Bacchae,* an almost Aeschylean play in both form and content that lies in total contrast to its recent predecessor *Orestes* (408) and the other surviving posthumous drama, *Iphigenia at Aulis.* In *Bacchae,* Dionysos gradually and inexorably takes a hideous vengeance on the human who has doubted his divinity; and he does so with even more severity than Athena in Sophocles' *Aias,* which had been created in the very different belief-climate of around thirty-five years earlier. By contrast, *Iphigenia at Aulis* is a drama of constant suspense – will Agamemnon's daughter be sacrificed or saved?

2.4 *Moira*

There is no predetermined fate or destiny in Greek tragedy.[21] The word *moira* is the nearest word the Greeks had to this concept; and it usually means a person's lot in life, though it is

---

[21]I am aware that in saying this I may be going against the pronouncement of the editors of the recent Cambridge Greek Lexicon, which offers 'lot, destiny, fate' as the second most important of the sixteen meanings given for *moira,* after the primary meaning 'lot' or 'share'. 'Destiny' or 'fate' are virtually unavoidable approximations in English translation, but it needs to be understood that the 'destiny' is not predetermined. I do not know how to convey this to an audience.

often used to mean his or her death. Understanding of *moira* could well begin with a famous passage in Homer's *Iliad*, where the Trojan hero Hektor, about to go into battle against the Greeks, attempts to soothe his wife, Andromache:

> Strange one, do not grieve overmuch for me;
> for nobody will hurl me to Hades beyond my *aisa*;[22]
> but I say that no one has escaped from his *moira*,
> coward or brave man, once it has first taken shape.
> Return to our house, go on with your work.

(6. 486–90)

The concept expressed here is crucial to the understanding not just of Homer but of Aeschylus and middle-period Sophocles. A person's *moira* is not fixed, but is inexorable *once it has taken shape*.[23] (There is nothing tragic about a poem or play such as Sartre's *Huis Clos* or Beckett's *Endgame*, in which the characters' fate is predetermined, and they are doomed before the action begins; this is nihilism. Predestination precludes tragedy.) These tragedies present examples of how a *moira* gradually takes shape, and the range of possibilities at the beginning narrows towards a climax where a tragic outcome *has become* inevitable. For example, in Aeschylus' *Seven against Thebes*, the action unfolds freely chosen to the point where Eteokles recognizes and accepts the curse of Oidipous, and sees that he must fight his brother Polyneikes at the seventh gate; he implacably resists the pleas of the Women of Thebes not to do this, and exits after speaking the chilling line: 'When

---

[22]*Aisa* is a synonym in Homer for *moira*.

[23]Hektor's *moira* takes shape in Book 16 of the *Iliad*, when he kills Achilleus' closest friend, Patroklos. Achilleus then resolves that he will avenge Patroklos by killing Hektor, even if this means his death – which it does, for it is Achilleus' own *moira* to die soon after Hektor (see his colloquy with his goddess mother Thetis, 18: 70ff.).

gods inflict it, you cannot escape from harm' (719).[24] In *Libation Bearers*, the matricide is by no means inevitable from the start of the play, and, in fact, Orestes' success hangs on a knife-edge during the scenes set in front of the palace; but when he has killed Aigisthos and confronts his mother, it has now become inevitable; Orestes' reply to Klytaimestra's warning clinches it:

> **Klytaimestra** Watch out! Beware your mother's angry, hounding Furies.
> **Orestes** But how should I escape my father's Furies, if I do not do this deed?
> **Klytaimestra** It seems as if I'm weeping uselessly, while still alive, before my tomb.
> **Orestes** Yes, now my father's fate wafts death towards you.
> **Klytaimestra** Oh god, this is the snake I bore, and nurtured at my breast.
> **Orestes** How true a prophet was that fearful dream. You killed, and it was wrong; now suffer wrong.
>
> (924ff.)[25]

Middle-period Sophoclean drama is very similar. Aias' death is not inevitable until he has of his own will left his tent during the period of Athena's wrath; Kreon in *Antigone* brings disaster on himself and his family by his incorrect response to a warning given by the gods through their prophet Teiresias; even Oidipous, who has killed his father and married his

---

[24]Cf. Ewans 1996a: xxxvii. Note also how in Dareios' speech in *Persians*, quoted above, Xerxes impetuously and freely brought a prophecy down upon himself and his empire.

[25]I demonstrated in Ewans 1980 the gradual movement in each of the three plays of the *Oresteia* towards a climax, two thirds of the way through the play, which by then has become inevitable.

mother long before *Oidipous the King* begins, brings his *moira* of recognition of those previously unknown facts down upon himself by his own relentlessly pursued inquiry into the death of Laios. And Herakles' death in *Women of Trachis*, though as we have seen it fulfils an ambiguous oracle given by Zeus at Dodona, nonetheless comes about through the freely chosen response of Deianeira to the importation into her house of his new mistress, Iole. Deianeira sent her husband, as a gift, a garment that she had smeared unknowingly with a deadly poison, believing it to be a love-charm that will enable her to regain his affection.

Neither the late plays of Sophocles (*Elektra, Philoktetes* and *Oidipous at Kolonos*), nor the majority of Euripides' surviving tragedies work in this way. In the late-fifth century, as previously noted, belief in the gods was being questioned. In Euripides' *Hecuba* (performed around 424), Troy has fallen, and the herald Talthybios enters to bring Hecuba an account of the bravery of her daughter Polyxena, whom the Greeks sacrificed as an offering at the tomb of Achilleus. He finds the former Queen of Troy lying in the dust, prostrate with grief, and, far from seeing in this spectacle any Aeschylean workings of divine *dikē* in the fall of Troy, he reacts as follows:

> Oh Zeus, what should I say? Do you look down
> on mortal men, or is that just a reputation which is false,
> and blind Chance oversees the whole of human life?
> This was the Queen of golden Troy,
> this was the wife of Priam, blessed with great prosperity.
> Now her city has been sacked,
> and she's an old slave woman with no children, lying on
> the ground, befouling her poor head with dirt.

(488–96)

Polyxena was sacrificed because the winds were blowing onshore, preventing the Greeks from returning home; the ghost of Achilleus allegedly appeared in golden armour over his tomb and protested that he has been denied due honour.

But, after the barbaric human sacrifice, the winds did not immediately fall still; that they finally change near the end of the play seems more because of chance than to the success of the sacrifice. Talthybios' speech questions the whole existence of the gods (or at least their relevance, if they do exist, to human beings), in a way that had not been seen in earlier tragedy; and this is not surprising at a time when war, plague and civil strife within *poleis* made men acutely aware of the fact that irreversible changes of fortune, usually from good to bad, could happen in a single day, and worshipping the gods seemed to many to be pointless.[26] If there are no gods (or if there are gods, but they do not intervene in human life), and Chance rules the world, then the older story-patterns in which a *moira* gradually takes shape to an outcome, which in retrospect is seen as inevitable, no longer have credibility. This makes possible a drama such as Euripides' extraordinary *Trojan Women* (415), which is also set, like *Hecuba,* after the sack of the city and before the Greeks' departure with their new female slaves. The previously opposed gods, Athena and Poseidon, agree at the outset that the fleet will suffer disaster on the voyage home, since the Greeks have offended both of them; but after that we see the women of Troy, both the anonymous individuals of the choros and members of the former Trojan royal family – Hecuba, Andromache and Kassandra – living out the action of a play that is virtually without a plot or a coherent sequence of events; it focuses instead on the women's ever-worsening sufferings in a timeless no-man's land that is almost prophetic of Samuel Beckett's *Waiting for Godot* (without the laughs).

Other plays from this period are not quite so radical in their dramaturgy; but, for example, both Sophocles' *Philoktetes* (409) and Euripides' *Orestes* (408) are full of sudden reversals of fortune, twists and turns in the plot; and both become so unexpected in the direction towards which they are heading

---

[26]Cf. Thucydides' analysis in *Histories* II: 52–3.

near the end of the play that a demigod (Herakles in *Philoktetes*) or a god (Apollo in *Orestes*) needs to intervene to restore the 'proper' outcome dictated by the traditional myth. Until Herakles appears on high, Neoptolemos is about to take Philoktetes from the island of Lemnos, not to Troy, where he is needed to enable the victory of the Greeks, but back to his homeland. And the situation near the end of *Orestes* calls for an even more drastic divine intervention. Orestes is preventing Menelaos from storming the doors of the palace on whose roof he is standing, by holding his sword to the throat of Menelaos' daughter Hermione. Apollo appears on the *mēchanē* (together with Helen, whom Orestes and Pylades think they have murdered; the gods have miraculously saved her from death); among other pronoucements, Apollo tells Orestes to put down the sword and marry the girl whom he is threatening to kill. The passions and hatreds of all the characters earlier in the play have driven the action so far away from the legendary course of events after the death of Klytaimestra that Apollo needs to appear on high to reimpose the traditional outcome 'by means of a solution so inadequate and so unreal by contrast with the created reality of the play that it is doomed into insignificance'.[27] It is hard not to believe that Apollo's intervention is to be viewed ironically, and should be played in a way that makes this plain.[28]

2.5 Comedy

Comedy had no inhibition about sending up the gods; it is fascinating to contrast the terrifying Dionysos of Euripides' posthumous *Bacchae* (406) with the cowardly buffoon of

---

[27]Arrowsmith 1958: 110.

[28]In their Santa Cruz production *Orestes Terrorist* (2011), Mary-Kay Gamel and director Danny Scheie brought out excellently the total implausibility of Apollo's imposed 'solution' to the outcome towards which the play was heading.

Aristophanes' *Frogs*, which was first performed in 405. And in *Birds* the human hero Pisthetairos threatens the messenger-goddess Iris with sexual assault, and then deprives Zeus himself of his power in the finale. Only Athena, patron goddess of the city, appears to be immune from the humour that is generated in many of the plays at the gods' expense; and Aristophanic comedy, with its anarchic inventions strung together on a fantasy-idea in a way that can hardly be described as a coherent plot in any normal sense of those words, is totally at odds with earlier tragedy's reflections on *moira* and divine causation.

2.6 Modern performance

I have indicated in **2.1** how modern performers can respond to the differences between Ancient Greek and modern Western values; it remains to outline strategies for coping with the basis of tragedy in myth, the presence of the gods and *daimones*, and the sense of a *moira* taking shape that is the basis for the surviving tragedies of Aeschylus and middle-period Sophocles.

Programme notes can provide our audiences with information about important events that have happened before the action begins, e.g. the expedition to and sack of Troy before the action of Euripides' *Hecuba, Trojan Women* and *Andromache*. They could also outline some previous versions of the myth being rehandled in a new play. Sometimes, however, even the Athenian audience was left in the dark; Aristotle records that Agathon wrote a tragedy called *Antheus* in which all the characters were fictitious, and I am among those who are convinced that Sophocles invented Antigone and Ismene to create a new story of Antigone's conflict with Kreon over the body of Polyneikes.[29] The technique of the 'intrusive gloss' might also be useful in helping audiences to understand the

---

[29]*Antheus*; Aristotle *Poetics* 51b20–5; *Antigone* Ewans 1999: xlv–xlvii, cf. Steiner 1983: 87.

story of a tragedy; a few extra well-chosen words can supply them with information about a character or a situation with whom or which the original audience was thoroughly familiar.

In Greek tragedy, with certain exceptions, the gods must be treated seriously. The American Repertory Theatre staged a production of the *Oresteia* in which the gods, on their appearance in *Eumenides,* were played for laughs;[30] that is to destroy any hope of conveying the meaning(s) of the trilogy to an audience. The Greek gods and *daimones* represent powers in and over human life that did not disappear with the demise of Graeco-Roman polytheism; for example, love, violence, chastity and childbirth, panic and ecstasy remain potent forces even though they are no longer embodied in their respective goddesses and gods Aphrodite, Ares, Artemis, Pan and Dionysos. And the *daimones* listed above on p. 49 are real powers in modern life as in ancient society. On occasion, it is good to gloss, e.g. by replacing 'Aphrodite' by 'the love goddess'; in an adequately gripping production of a Greek drama, a few such devices are sufficient, when the play is acted with conviction, to enable modern audiences to enter imaginatively into a world in which gods and goddesses were important powers, to be worshipped and propitiated. For example, Euripides' *Hippolytos* and *Bacchae* demand absolute belief in the power of the gods who appear in them, a power that is demonstrated in the action of the plays. Well directed, even the first scene of Sophocles' *Aias,* in which Athena torments her victim in the presence of Odysseus (whom the deluded Aias cannot see) can be a convincing, indeed a powerfully effective, piece of theatre for a modern audience unaccustomed to the appearance of supernatural powers in serious drama. But the divine element in Greek tragedy has been subjected to brilliant comic send-ups, as for example in *Up Pompeii!* and the parody of the *deus ex machina* at the end of Joe Orton's *What the Butler Saw,* so the task is not an easy one.

---

[30]Goldhill 2007: 212–14. He rightly condemned this production.

Seamus Heaney could not accommodate Herakles' speech setting to right the action of *Philoktetes* in his version *The Cure at Troy*, remarking that: 'I simply had not the nerve to bring on a god two minutes from curtain.'[31] Instead, he deploys a volcanic eruption, and a member of his small chorus *ritually clamant, as Hercules* resolves the tensions that the plot has created.[32] This is arguably not a solution; it remains the fact that divine intervention is needed, in Heaney's play as in Sophocles'. Philoktetes has refused to go back to Troy, even to lead the Greek conquest of the city – a refusal that has been adamant up until Herakles' intervention. Perhaps the problem in this particular play is insoluble. In the case of *Hippolytos* and *Bacchae*, we need to 'crash through or crash', presenting the authority of Aphrodite (and of Artemis, who appears at the end of *Hippolytos* to redress the balance) and Dionysos with all the power at the actors' disposal, and hoping that the modern audience will be induced to suspend disbelief enough to understand the awesome power that they wield, as personified representatives of forces that still affect human life in the modern world. Much easier to handle are the divine appearances at the end of such plays as Euripides' *Elektra* and *Orestes*; as we have already seen (**2.4** on *Orestes*) those interventions were undoubtedly intended to be taken ironically by the original audience, and can easily be played that way in a modern performance.

I have given examples above of the fact that there is a gradual development in the tragedies of Aeschylus and middle-period Sophocles from an ominous initial starting point via a period during which a *moira* takes shape to the climax – an action that at that point in time has become inevitable.[33] This

---

[31]Quoted in Goldhill 2007: 205.

[32]Heaney 1990: 78–9.

[33]This usually occurs around two thirds of the way through the play, with the remainder devoted to exploring the consequences. Contrast the abrupt ending of many Elizabethan and Jacobean tragedies almost immediately after the bloody climax, with order re-established tentatively (as, e.g. in *Hamlet*), or not at all (*King Lear*).

needs careful handling in modern productions. The director and actors should identify the points at which clues are laid to the direction in which the action is tending, and make sure that these are emphasized to the audience. For example, in *Agamemnon* the main development is the ever-increasing 'masculine' power of Klytaimestra, observed even by the Watchman in Scene 1 and demonstrated in successive scenes by her interactions with the Elders, the Herald and Agamemnon himself. Meanwhile, the destruction of the gods' altars and temples at Troy, and its punishment by the gods' sending a mighty storm that destroyed much of the Greek fleet and scattered the surviving ships, has been explored in Scenes 2 and 3 as a further indication that Aeschylus' gods inflict severe penalties on those who offend them. And the Elders' meditations in Choroses 1, 2 and 3, starting with their description of the horrific sacrifice of Iphigenia and culminating in a denunciation of wealthy houses with a background of crime (750ff.), which immediately precedes Agamemnon's entry in his chariot, are ominous in the extreme for the king. That is followed by his entrance into the palace, walking over the robes on which a mere mortal should not trample (**3.4.1.4**), and then by Kassandra's revelations about the bloodstained past of the House of Atreus (**3.5.2.3**). At that point his death has become inevitable and imminent. All these developing threads must be brought out when staging the movement to Agamemnon's death, the climax of Aeschylus' extraordinary masterpiece. And similar threads, leading up to the point where a *moira* becomes inevitable, can and must be traced – and emphasized in production – in the other surviving plays of Aeschylus and in middle-period Sophocles.

Matters are very different in the plays of Sophocles and especially Euripides from after around 425; their unexpected changes of direction and unpredictable plotlines have a different focus, not on how a deeply expected act becomes inevitable, but on offering the audience, both ancient and modern, the suspense of wondering *what* is going to happen next. It is arguable that these dramas are easier to play today, since this kind of plot-pattern is naturally much more frequent in contemporary drama than the earlier, *moira*-based one; and their vision of a world full of ruthlessly amoral individuals, which occasionally goes beyond deep cynicism (Euripides' *Andromache*, Sophocles' *Philoktetes*) to verge upon a completely pessimistic view of human life (Sophocles' *Elektra*, Euripides' *Hecuba* and *Trojan Women*), may quite easily resonate with audiences living in our times, where pessimism and cynicism are justifiably shared by many members of society.

3

Performing Greek Plays on the Modern Stage

3.1 Translation

3.1.1 Introduction

It is often said that casting is the most important decision that a director must make; but arguably for a foreign-language play, the choice of translation is even more important. There is of course no such thing as a perfect translation of a Greek verse play around 2,450 years old; but there are certain criteria. George Steiner's massive essay on language and translation, *After Babel*,[1] demanded that good translation should attempt the impossible – a synthesis of literal fidelity to the source text, and literate expression in the target language. Ancient Greek has a grammar and syntax that are very different from those of modern English; and the challenge of the Greek dramas to the contemporary translator is to be as *accurate* as possible (this is not the same as being literal), while also providing *actable* versions that enable a poetic drama to be played before audiences that have no live tradition of verse plays. If these two criteria – accuracy and actability – are pursued

---

[1]Steiner 1975: Chapter 4 *passim*.

simultaneously, a creative tension results, which is very fruitful. Along with fellow Drama Professors Graham Ley and Gregory McCart, and my PhD student Jessica Alexander-Lillicrap, I have adopted this working method; and we have tested the resulting translations in workshop or full performance before publication, modifying any wording that proved cumbersome or inadequate on the rehearsal floor.[2]

Unfortunately, there are several translations of Greek drama that are clearly unactable (one can only wonder if the authors even read them aloud, let alone workshopped and/or performed them before publication). Emerita Prof. Mary-Kay Gamel (University of California Santa Cruz) and I both became translators because we were invited to work on productions of Greek tragedies and found that we could not recommend any of the then published translations for theatre use. That situation has improved in the past forty years; but translations are still published that are quite pedestrian and unsuitable for acting. On the other hand, there are also very loose translations, often described as 'a version by' or 'adapted by' that are excessively free from the meaning(s) of the original Greek. I cannot recommend these, because Aeschylus, Sophocles, Euripides and Aristophanes were all consummate poets in their own right (writing in four very different styles); the imagery and power of their masterpieces does not require intrusive modifications to be accessible to modern audiences.[3] The National Theatre of Great Britain commissioned the well-known poet Ted Hughes to write a 'version' of the *Oresteia* for Katie Mitchell's 1999 production; it contained verses such as the following:

---

[2]For the published translations using this method cf. Works Cited, Ewans (tr.) or (ed.) entries. Jessica's translations of Euripides' *Iphigenia Among the Taurians* and *Helen* are contained in her thesis (see Works Cited under Alexander-Lillicrap).

[3]Menander is not in the same league as the fifth-century dramatists for richness of verse; he partially makes up for this, however, by his insights into human nature.

> (**Herald**)   We suffered in the ships, tortured by boredom
>   and lice,
>   by the stench, sodden with sweat, vomit, urine –
>   sleep a cramp of agony, tumbled in storms –
>   and on land the dog-holes were worse.
>   The stench, the rats, the cockroaches, worse,
>   filthy with fleas and dysentery,
>   crutches raw and bleeding, we dug in
>   under the enemy's wall. We lived there
>   pelted with their ordure,
>   or made our beds in the salt marsh
>   with the crabs and mosquitoes.
>   Our finger-joints clubbed with rheumatism,
>   icy or streaming with fever.
>   In every ten men, nine were trembling.
>   Then, god help us, the winter.
>   The wind off those white peaks.
>   Toes fell off, birds dropped out of the trees.
>   A man's back could snap if he bent of a sudden.
>   Then in midsummer the heat – the heat!
>   The sea was a puddle of lead.
>   The earth too hot for the bare footsole.
>   The touch of bronze blistered.[4]

Compare this with my attempt to convey what Aeschylus actually wrote:

---

[4]Hughes 1999: 30, reproduced with permission from Faber and Faber. Ben Power's *Medea* (c. 2015, also for the National Theatre) is just one other example of a free adaptation. One wonders why major companies think that the original tragedies, in accurate translations, would be too difficult for their audiences to appreciate. For a counter-example of a 'new version' that closely parallels the original cf. Frank McGuiness' *Hecuba* (2004). And Seamus Heaney's *The Burial at Thebes* (2005, after *Antigone*) is an example of a great poet disciplining himself to follow the gist of his source text, while introducing contemporary references into his choruses.

(**Herald**)   Suppose I told you of our sufferings – bad
    quarters,   555
  narrow gangways, lousy bedding – what did we not
  complain about? Each day brought every form of
    misery.
  Then when we landed things were even worse;
  we had to sleep close under hostile walls;
  and from the heavens and the meadowland   560
  dew drizzled down on us, a constant plague
  making our woollen garments verminous.
  And then the winter, death to all bird life,
  intolerable cold brought by the snows of Ida –
  or scorching heat, when the sea fell asleep,   565
  a noon siesta without wind or wave.[5]

The extra detail in Hughes' 'version' is self-indulgence by a
poet who is used to the written word and does not possess
Aeschylus' mastery of dramatic form or his understanding of
the virtue of economy. In 1978, Oliver Taplin delivered a
polemic against such translations, and against directors who
show ignorance or wilful disregard of the dramatic technique
of the playwrights whose work they are reviving;[6] his key
words about translation are that: 'the ... translator tries to
transfer into his language what he thinks is essential in the
original, and his success or failure depends both on his choice
of what is essential and on his ability to convey that essence.'[7]
Hughes has no care to reproduce that 'essence'; in an attempt
(presumably) to achieve extra vividness, the modern poet's
expansion and gross exaggerations destroy Aeschylus'
compact, and as a result, very powerful evocation of the
soldiers' sufferings (twelve lines to Hughes' twenty-two!). I

---

[5]Ewans 1995: 18.
[6]Taplin 1978: 172–81.
[7]1978: 180. We will return to what Taplin wrote about directing tragedy in
3.2.2.

vastly prefer Aeschylus' original metaphor for the scorching heat of summer, 565–6, to Hughes' 'puddle of lead'.

3.1.2 Desiderata

The medium for a modern translation of a poetic drama that is designed to be acted must be verse. (Unfortunately, Oxford University Press has published versions of Greek tragedy in which the spoken dialogue is rendered in prose, as it is in the Penguin Aristophanes.)[8] Verse translation is essential, since the translator must attempt to match the poetic power of the original Greek text, and to reflect the different kinds of verse that were used in the plays (see **3.3–5**). A prose translation is diminished in power simply by being in prose, since the actors will be unaware of, and so unable to respond to, a key difference between these texts and modern spoken prose plays. However, Ancient Greek verse was a pattern of alternating long and short syllables, often in complex combinations; since modern English verse does not use such patterns, but only a stress accent, attempting to reproduce them is not appropriate.[9]

Greek plays, both tragedy and comedy, alternate between dialogue lines – predominantly six-foot and occasionally eight-foot – and much shorter lines in the anapaests and lyrics. Like several other translators, I have found that a five- or six-stress English line works well for dialogue, and a three- to four-stress line for lyrics. Occasionally, where the Greek is extremely concise, it is possible to reduce these lengths by one stress, and sometimes an expansion is needed. But it is important to match the concision of the ancient texts; they are rich but economical, and it is unfortunate that there are many translations that use

---

[8]The prose versions in the Loeb Classical Library and Aris and Philips editions of the Greek texts are however more than acceptable; there the editor uses prose simply to elucidate the meaning of the original, as he or she sees it, as literally and directly as possible.

[9]It also leads to constraints on what can be written, which leads inevitably to unacceptable freedom from the meaning of the original Greek. Cf. e.g. Neuburg 1992.

more lines than the Greek original.[10] English does not have to be more verbose than Greek!

The qualities that make a translation of these texts actable are *rhythm* and *flow*. As in the original Greek dramas, a steady pulse needs to underlie the verse, to enable a good delivery; similarly a constant flow – except of course in scenes of high excitement – helps the actor to be confident in delivering his or her part. Infelicities of English expression and archaisms need to be avoided; and clarity must be aimed at even – or perhaps especially – in the more densely complex passages of tragic choral lyric that are common in Aeschylus and to a lesser extent in Sophocles and Euripides. This must not, however, come at the cost of a loss of fidelity. Directors who choose translations adhering to these principles will have a much easier time when they come to the rehearsal room.

3.1.3 Comedy

Aristophanes' comedies were one-off performances that freely referenced named living individuals and events current in the year of production. They also abound in references to Athenian institutions, such as cults, which are obscure today. The scholarly translations respond to this with footnotes, sometimes well over 100 for a play of 1,200 to 1,600 lines. But nobody can act a footnote, so a translation that has as one of its prime aims to be actable, has to adopt a different strategy. I have called this process evoking the *effective meaning* of the problematic piece of text.[11] For example, *Lysistrata* begins with the following (in a literal translation):

Lysistrata (*alone*) But if someone had summoned them to a place of bacchic revelry, or [a grotto of] Pan or to

---

[10]For example, Svarlien's 2008 *Medea*, and most of the translations of individual tragedies in the OUP New York series.
[11]Ewans 2010: 43–5.

> Kolias or [a shrine of] Genetyllis,
> you wouldn't be able to move for all the wild
>   drumming.
> As it is, there's not a single woman here.

Line two, if presented like this, needs three footnotes, and in most translations that is exactly what you get. But this is hopeless for performance, so the translator must first know exactly what kind of celebrations Aristophanes was evoking,[12] and then bring the effective meaning of what Lysistrata is saying before a modern audience:

> **Lysistrata** (*alone*)   But if someone had summoned them
>   for an orgy,
>   or a sleep-out or a celebration of the love goddess,
>   you wouldn't be able to move for all the wild
>   drumming.
>   As it is, there's not a single woman here.[13]

Aristophanic verse has a very wide range of expression – from the truly lyrical via both parody of the high tragic style and the freely conversational, to crisp exchanges that are often the vehicle for a slapstick comedy routine. This demands a great deal of flexibility – and of course there is this poet's famed bawdiness; do not use a translation that resorts to euphemisms. When Aristophanes says 'fuck', 'bugger', 'prick' or 'cunt' – as he often does – he means it! (Incidentally these and other 'obscenities' – a Roman, not a Greek word – are used for their anatomical exactitude. They were never employed as swear words; the Greeks swore only by the gods.)

Aristophanes has three further traps for the would-be translator and director. The first is for the translator; the

---

[12]For these see Henderson 1987: 66–7 or 1996: 208–9.
[13]Ewans 2010: 55.

playwright sometimes uses Greek puns that are almost always impossible to recreate in English. I reluctantly believe that most of these need to be either completely reframed, or omitted from performance.[14] Then there is the question of dialect; people in Aristophanes who come from regions other than the Athenian territory of Attika naturally speak in Aristophanes' approximation of the dialects used in, for example, Sparta, Megara and Boiotia. Some translators, centred on South-East England, have rendered their speeches into, for example, Scottish or Irish dialect, while WASP translators in the northern parts of the USA have in the past used 'southern' idioms. This is no longer acceptable, as we have come to recognize the equality and importance of diverse cultures inside our nation-states. In my translations, I have left all the speeches of the dialect speakers in the same standard Australian English as the Athenian characters, leaving it to directors, if they will, to mark off the people from elsewhere in Greece in some other way (e.g. by costume?). There is a related problem with the mock-barbarian dialogue of the Scythian policeman in *The Women's Festival* and the barbarian god Triballos in *Birds,* both of whom speak mangled Greek. Again, I have left it to the director to choose whether, and if so how, to differentiate them from the Greek characters in the play.

Finally, there is the problem of 'political correctness'. Several of Aristophanes' comedies portray girls and young women as sex objects, to the point where in an earlier wave of feminism in the USA it was felt that the gender politics of Ancient Athens are so remote from due recognition of the equality, which women rightly demand in modern Western democracies, that women should not consent to act in classical Greek plays. Sue-Ellen Case even hoped that 'feminist practitioners and scholars may decide that such plays do not belong in the canon'.[15]

---

[14]For an example of a series of puns (in *Knights*) and a possible way to treat them cf. Ewans 2011: 32–3.

[15]1988: 19. Cf. Taaffe 1993: 146.

There are some scenes in Aristophanes that make many of us uncomfortable today, for example, the sub-scene in *Peace* (877ff.), where the Second Slave is fondling the body of the nubile young goddess Festival. Trygaios orders her to take off all her clothes, and he then offers her up to the Council Executive to be fucked in all sorts of different ways, which he details before handing her to a VIP in the front row.

I think we have to make an uncompromising choice; take it or leave it. We cannot impose our own values on a play from the past; what would happen to *The Merchant of Venice* if we sought to present it without its fundamental premise that a Jew's religion is to be despised, and he must be converted to Christianity for his own salvation, by force if necessary? It simply cannot be done, and in my view should not be attempted. *Peace* is one long ode to release after the long sufferings of a ten-year war, and fucking is one of the many blessings that the male characters dream of in the comedy. These are facts and should not be denied or downplayed. Carl Caulfield, the professional actor who played Trygaios in my production, rightly remarked that the real obscenity is not sexuality but war, with its deaths and permanent injuries. *Peace* is an excellent play, and deserves to be staged without censorship.

There is no need to insert new jokes into a translation. Aristophanes was a great comic poet, and he provides, with his own material, both verbal humour and a rich area for exploration in *lazzi* (comic routines) in modern production. For an example of such a comic routine, study the Empousa scene in *Frogs* (271ff.), with the detailed blocking, based on workshop experimentation, given below in **3.4.2.2.** Directors and actors will find much to discover in the scripts, if they are translated with accuracy and actability foremost in the translator's mind, and the translation provides enough 'hooks' – specific expressive words that actors can use as a basis for developing physical gestures and movements to illuminate the text.

3.2 Setting, costumes and masks

3.2.1 'Ancient' or modern?[16]

Several famous productions have sought to solemnize and ritualize Greek tragedy; two different examples would be the *Oresteia* directed by Peter Hall in 1981 and *Les Atrides* (1990), in which Ariane Mnouchkine presented the *Oresteia* preceded by Euripides' *Iphigenia at Aulis* (a jarring combination, since Euripides' posthumous play of 406 is very different in its values and vision from Aeschylus' trilogy of 458). In Hall's production, there were all-male actors; heavy, elaborate costumes; a slow delivery of the text; an extensive use of music even in dialogue scenes; stylized gestures and masks (which in an indoor theatre can only have a distancing effect on the audience, the reverse of their original function at Athens). Mnouchkine's production was far more energetic; but she too used elaborate costumes and Kathakali make-up, which gives a mask-like effect. Both directors sought to establish Greek tragedy as a solemn ritual experience, far removed from the rapid cut and thrust of much contemporary Western drama and from the reality of the audience's daily lives.

This is problematic. Greek tragedy and comedy were indeed parts of a religious festival (though the worship of Dionysos, with its phallic processions and ecstatic celebrations, was far from most modern Western conceptions of 'religion'); but they were not themselves acts of ritual. They were competitive dramas, designed to involve the spectators with the characters and their fortunes. Nothing that I can see in the scripts evokes ritual solemnity; on the contrary, these are dynamic dramas, tragedies that are designed to move their audiences to strong emotions, and comedies that seek to make them enjoy themselves and laugh. Bury them in a ritualistic production and

---

[16]I place 'ancient' in inverted commas because such productions rarely reflect with any degree of exactitude the actual costumes and masks that the Greeks used for dramatic performances (for which see above **1.5**).

you are simply presenting a spectacle – perhaps impressive in itself, but not successful in engaging the feelings of the modern audience with the emotions and meanings of the original text. I therefore prefer productions that are dynamic and unmasked, as in modern indoor productions masks *conceal* rather than *reveal,* unless the actors are highly trained in mask work.

In my first production (*Libation Bearers,* 1983), I used 'ancient' costume; but, on reflection, I decided that the production was not wholly successful – partly because I was too influenced by other people's ideas on how to perform the choros parts, but mostly because the 'ancient' costumes were unsatisfactory.[17] Subsequently, I adopted modern dress for my productions of both tragedy and comedy, since it enables the audience to understand individuals in ways that cannot be shown using 'ancient' – or for that matter 'timeless' – costumes. (The Greeks themselves used contemporary dress, cf. **1.5.**)

In the case of two tragedies I went further, and made direct allusion to recent events. I described my 1996 *Antigone* as set in 'Thebes c. 1200 BCE/Sarajevo 1994'. Kreon was a leather-jacketed warlord in his forties, much younger than the aged patriarch presented in some productions; he went nowhere without a sizeable bodyguard toting a sub-machine gun, who later became the dishevelled Messenger bringing back the tragic news of the deaths of Antigone and Haimon. I chose Bosnia not only because of the siege, but also because it is a Muslim nation; women are expected to be much more decorous and less assertive than is the norm in most Northern European nations, North America and of course Australia. So Ismene's reticence and Kreon's blatant misogyny made sense, and both

---

[17]For example, I had to exaggerate Aigisthos' character by costuming him in an exceedingly decadent way, to contrast with the plain, black dresses worn by the Libation Bearers themselves. Similarly, the National Theatre of Greece's 1998 'classical' *Medea* (see Appendix) removed all ambiguity or complexity from the character of the title figure, by clothing the Nurse and Tutor in black, the Women of Corinth in white and Medea herself in a striking red dress. Modern dress, especially for female characters, brings with it many subtle codes that the director and costume designer can use to their advantage.

Ismene and Eurydike wore full-length dresses and hijabs. Antigone by contrast wore jeans and a short-sleeved blouse, and signalled her defiance of male-dominated convention by having only a flimsy headscarf that she tossed over her hair when leaving to bury Polyneikes. The resulting production enabled our audiences to reflect on parallels between Sophocles' drama and contemporary life; but above all it allowed them to become closely involved with the characters and their fate.

In 1997 I presented in a natural amphitheatre with ocean views an open-air production of Sophocles' *Aias*; the play is set in and near the Greek camp besieging Troy, where a coalition of leaders from various Greek city-states had brought their armies together by sea to support Agamemnon and Menelaos. It was irresistible to evoke in our modern-dress production the international coalition that deployed in Iraq during the First Gulf War. Viewing the play from an Australian perspective, Aias himself and his choros of Sailors naturally became an Australian naval commander and his men; Odysseus – who is first presented as Aias' bitter enemy – was represented as a Frenchman, reflecting the great dislike of the French at this time in Australasia because of the Moruroa nuclear tests and the 1985 bombing of the *Rainbow Warrior* in Auckland Harbour; and Agamemnon and Menelaos became arrogant American five-star generals. Tekmessa was an Arabian captive princess, in a suitably exotic costume. Uniforms for each of the nationalities were exact, as were their accents. The setting once again, as with *Antigone*, served to bring the emotions of the drama over to the modern audience in a way that would be impossible in a masked 'ancient' performance.[18] And the fluid style of the translation was perfect for the very realistic style of the production.[19]

---

[18]Working in California, Mary-Kay Gamel set her 2011 *Ajax* in Vietnam for similar reasons to mine.

[19]Although my translations were all designed for unmasked performance, it is fascinating that Chris Vervain used them successfully in her 2016 masked indoor productions in London of *Libation Bearers* and *Eumenides*. But viewing the DVDs I feel there is a tension between the involvement that my scripts encourage and the distancing effect of masks in a small theatre.

In other productions, such as the 1998 Sophocles *Elektra* and the three Aristophanes comedies that I took to full production (*Lysistrata* 2005, *The Women's Festival* 2006 and *Peace* 2009), I simply used modern dress. The costumes were designed to help each actor to inhabit their character without an overall production concept evoking a specific place and date. For example, in *Lysistrata* Lampito the athletic Spartan wore a white sports dress, while the cock-teasing Myrrhine (whose name alludes to myrtle, which was a slang word for the vagina), wore a skimpy, low-cut blue blouse, a yellow miniskirt and yellow high heels.

Modern dress is of course expected and natural in contemporary adaptations, such as Northern Broadsides' 2007 *Lisa's Sex Strike*. But I believe that it works for close translations of the original Greek as well as for such free versions. Over eight such productions from 1985 to 2009 I had only one audience member complain that she expected 'classical' dress. And that complaint was for the 'Thebes/Sarajevo' *Antigone*, which played to packed houses for an unprecedented three weeks, drew parties of school students from up to five hours' drive away and received nothing but praise during the Q & A sessions that were held after all the matinees.

3.2.2 Desiderata

Some directors reading this book may think that the facts set out in Chapter One about the Ancient Athenian festivals, staging practices and conventions are not something that they need to know in order to create their own contemporary production. But this is not the case; Chapter One summarizes the essential information that a dramaturg should supply, and of which a director must be aware. To take a central example, an effective set for a production of Greek tragedy or comedy must have three entrances, one upstage centre through doors over a threshold, and one from each of the wings, echoing the *eisodoi* of the ancient stage. This is true whether you are lucky enough to have an arena configuration at your disposal, with an audience surrounding the action on three sides, or you have to stage your Greek play for an end-on audience, with or without a proscenium arch.[20] But just getting the basic configuration right is not enough. Oliver Taplin argued vigorously in 1978 that a knowledge of the staging techniques used by the Greeks is essential for the modern director. After illustrating many of these earlier in *Greek Tragedy in Action*, much of his final chapter is a polemic against 'creative' directors who think they know more about tragic stagecraft than the original playwrights, and this *Regietheater* approach has unfortunately proliferated even more in the subsequent forty-odd years (cf. the Introduction, above).[21] To quote one crucial passage:

> [In translation] unintentional failure to convey the creator's meaning may be inevitable; but it is still the director's task to do his best, and not deliberately to change, distort or 'improve'. Likewise in the sphere of visual meaning: he must try to elicit and present it by translation. The author's explicit and implicit stage directions should be given due emphasis. Moreover, the invention and interpolation of stage business, that is of visual meaning, must be shunned, because this replaces the author's meaning, and even when it does not positively contradict, it distracts and submerges and distorts. To most players of early music these imperatives would seem commonplace; to a modern director in the theatre they might appear intolerably restrictive. But are they? I see these as liberating constraints, limits within

---

[20]On directing and acting Greek drama on an end-on stage cf. below **3.6**.

[21]Taplin was also rightly hostile, on the other hand, to attempts to present 'replicas' of the ancient productions. Even if this were possible – and it is not, because of our lack of detailed knowledge – the audience of today is naturally not the same as the Ancient Greek audience. To see how disastrous such an attempt can be, cf. YouTube 'British Recreation of Greek Theatre: *Oedipus Rex* 1953' (actually a Canadian production) – an unfortunate example of what Peter Brook famously called 'the deadly theatre'.

which the interpreter may work all the better for knowing what it is he is interpreting. And there remains open all the variety that is the product of critical interpretation and scenic translation.[22]

Taplin would be less dogmatic these days, as he has seen many more productions, and worked as a dramaturg for professional directors; but he still '[remains] more likely to respond positively to productions that bring out the built-in theatricalities of the "original" play'.[23] And he deplores a tendency for *Regietheater* productions, in which the director imposes a 'concept' that very often does not harmonize at all with the play that is supposedly being presented, to bill themselves as, for example, 'Aeschylus' *Oresteia*', when in fact they are effectively presenting new works. I agree with him; performances that adapt the texts freely and inventively are to be encouraged, provided that they do not purport to be by a Greek playwright, but are billed as (for example) '*Bacchae*, adapted from Euripides by [author/director]' or '*Bacchae* by [author], after Euripides'.

Taplin's book was devoted to tragedy, but Aristophanes was also a master of the visual. As will be shown below (**3.4.2**), his comedies contain implicit stage business (lots of it), and ingenious use of props.

These plays do not need added gratuitous stage business and (in comedy) visual gags that are not justified by the text; all that is needed is there to be discovered by directors and actors working with and respecting the script. But in saying this I do not mean to imply that there is no room for interpretation. On the contrary, I am arguing that by using an accurate translation, and understanding the nature of the texts that the Greek dramatists created, your imagination will be liberated to create an interpretation that does not work against

---

[22]Taplin 1978: 179.
[23]Personal email to the author, 15 December 2020.

the plays but enhances them; in this way your production will be free to bring out the many contemporary echoes that these dramas can and must evoke in a modern audience, and you can reflect your own concerns without imposing an incongruous vision.

3.3 Speech and song

I have written in **1.8**, perhaps controversially, that Greek tragedy was realistic. Unlike comedy, it does not acknowledge the presence of the audience;[24] and it dramatizes scenes familiar from daily life, such as homecomings, recognitions, supplication, funeral rites and acts of violence.[25] But you may well ask how any medium can be described as realistic that incorporates as a fundamental component song and dance? Part of the answer lies in an aspect of the Ancient Greek language.

Greek was a pitch-accented language, like modern Chinese. This means that even the simplest spoken words become almost musical. I was once waiting for a plane in Singapore's Changi Airport when over the PA system came a beautiful succession of sounds that I could not understand from a female announcer, rising and falling in pitch in a deeply melodic way. Then came the translation, delivered on a monotone: 'Qantas announces the departure of flight QF 4 to Sydney.'

---

[24]The nearest a tragedy comes to this is when in Aeschylus' *Eumenides*, Athena delivers her speech founding the court of the Areopagos to 'our future citizens' (708) over the heads of the other characters in the playing space. Prologues and portions of messenger speeches are also directly addressed to the audience, though – importantly – this is not acknowledged. Contrast Dikaiopolis' address to the audience in the first speech of Aristophanes' *Acharnians* (NB. 41: 'Didn't I tell you?').

[25]Aristophanes' surviving comedies depend on fantasy ideas – but once the fantasy is established, everyone in the play behaves as if its world were completely real.

Being a pitch-accented language like Chinese, Ancient Greek, when spoken, was far nearer to the condition of song than any modern European language. So the move 'upwards', when the choros or a soloist switched from speech into song, accompanied only by the sound of the solo *aulos* (a double-reed woodwind instrument), was far smoother than the very abrupt transition in the modern Western musical between the unaccompanied spoken dialogue and the sung lyrics that are accompanied by a full orchestra or at least a band. And the pace of dramatic time is inevitably slowed by the performance of a song set to modern Western music. Think how much is necessarily cut by the librettist and/or the composer from plays that have been transformed into operas; consider, for example, Verdi's *Otello*, Strauss' *Salome* and Debussy's *Pelléas et Mélisande*, which all abbreviate the original plays by Shakespeare, Wilde and Maeterlinck to create operas with a manageable running time. This has implications for how we stage Greek drama today, especially for our treatment of the choros (see **3.5**).[26]

3.4 Acting

3.4.1 Tragedy

The actor in Greek tragedy is very exposed. The set is simply a façade behind you, and there are few props, either hand-held or pre-set in the playing space. You are not surrounded by walls, furniture and props in relation to which you can locate your character, as you are in a modern box set. And you may have long speeches to deliver as well as snappy dialogue in interaction with other actors. But these challenges can be overcome.

---

[26]Cf. also the discussion of some modern productions available on YouTube in the Appendix.

3.4.1.2 Solo speech

Let us look first at one substantial speech and elicit some strategies for performing it. Halfway through Aeschylus' *Agamemnon,* the king returns in a chariot from his victory at Troy (bringing with him his new concubine, Kassandra) and addresses his Elders, inviting them to celebrate the victory and stating his resolve to deal with any treachery or subversion that may have developed during his absence. He then prepares to leave the chariot and enter his palace. At this point, his wife Klytaimestra intervenes. In the text that follows, I have numbered the beginning of each new beat; this will help with our analysis.[27]

(**Agamemnon**)   Now I will go into my house,

Doors open. Enter **Klytaimestra** *from the palace, followed by Maidservants with robes.*[28]

and make beside the hearth first greeting to the gods,
who sent me out so far and led me back again.
Since victory has followed me, may it remain secure.

---

[27]Breaking text down into beats is of course a practice that goes back to Stanislavsky and Michael Chekhov. It has special value when working with long speeches in Greek drama.

[28]Taplin (1977: 307–8) and several others would have her enter immediately before 855. This would mean that she would deliver 855ff. from in front of the doorway. However, she needs to be beside and in front of the chariot before 855, both to prevent Agamemnon from leaving the chariot and to ensure that she can deliver the first four beats of the speech directly to the Elders, who will have retreated to FL as the chariot came in from the BR *eisodos* to C (cf. Ewans 1995: 144). If she began the speech from the doorway, she would not prevent Agamemnon from descending, and also would be in a very bad position to address the Elders, since the chariot at C and its horse would lie between her and them. (The chariot must stop at C, as in a devastating series of moves Klytaimestra converts Agamemnon's presence at the position of the greatest power in the playing space into a position where she has total control over him.) After gesturing to Agamemnon to remain in the chariot before 855, she begins her speech to the Elders immediately in front of it, at FC.

Klytaimestra (*with a gesture, she prevents Agamemnon
    from leaving the chariot*)
   1 Men of the city, Elders of Argos, I   855
am not ashamed to speak of how I love
my husband. Time erodes
all reticence. I have not learnt from others –
I shall tell you of my wretched life
for all the time this man was camped before the
    walls of Troy.   860
2 First, for a woman to remain at home
alone, without a man – that is unbearable;
she has to hear so many fresh and wounding
    rumours –
one herald comes, and then another brings a tale
    of woe
worse than the last, crying sorrow for the house.   865
3 Indeed, if this man here had suffered from
as many wounds as rumours said
which reached us, he'd have more holes in him
    than a net.
And if he'd died as many deaths as stories claimed
he'd be a second Geryon with three bodies   870
and he could boast that he had got a triple cloak
of earth, a death for each of his three shapes.
4 Because of all these wounding tales
they often had to hold me forcibly,
and free my neck from nooses I had strung from
    up above.   875
5 That's why your child's not standing here
as he should be, the guardian of the pledges made
by me and you, Orestes; do not be amazed;
our faithful ally's looking after him,   880
Strophios the Phokian. He alerted me in cautious
    words
to dangers on two sides; first, your peril in the war
at Troy, and then the chance that popular
revolt might hatch a wicked plot,

since men often give a further kick when one
    is down.   885
So this excuse of mine bears no deceit.

6 But as for me, the gushing fountains of my tears
have now run dry, and not one drop is left.
With waiting late at night my eyes are sore
as I cried bitterly because the beacons for your
    victory   890
always refused to light; and in my dreams
I was awakened by the gentle rushing of a gnat
buzzing aloud, since I saw you suffering more
than could have happened in the time sleep shared
    with me.

7 Now I've endured all that, with joyful heart   895
I would proclaim this man the watchdog of a
    farm,
the saving forestay of a ship, a high-roofed
    house's
solid pillar, or a father's only son,
to thirsty travellers a flowing spring,
and land for sailors suddenly in sight beyond   900
their hopes, a fair day dawning after storm.

> **Klytaimestra** *prostrates herself full-length on the
> ground before* **Agamemnon** *in homage. After a
> few moments she rises to her feet again.*

8 These are the words in which I think it right to
    honour him:
may Jealousy stand far away; we have endured
    so much
before. **9** And now, my dear beloved, step   905
out of this chariot – but don't permit your foot
to touch the ground, my king, the foot that
    conquered Troy.
Women, why do you wait? I have instructed you
to clothe the area with fabrics where he has to walk.

The Maidservants strew robes between the palace
doors and the chariot.

Create at once a crimson path, where Justice may   910
lead him into a house he never sought to see.
All else a mind not overcome by sleep
will justly make, with gods' help, reach the fated end.

This speech is so long that in his reply Agamemnon curtly compares it to the length of time he spent at Troy, and also says that praise should not come from her but from others, and that it should be modest (914–17). (The speech is indeed a stunning and extended display of rhetoric, in a manner considered by the Greeks to be deeply unsuitable for a woman.) This picks up what the Elders had said before Klytaimestra entered; greeting Agamemnon when he entered at 782, they questioned what the due measure of praise for him should be – neither too great nor too small. They also warned that the king should look closely at the citizens back home, to see: 'which . . . has acted justly, and which has misused his time' (808–9).

These are the important clues to what Klytaimestra is doing. She is deceiving on the grandest scale both the Elders and above all Agamemnon, in preparation to murder him by surprise entrapment; she is also lauding him with grossly exaggerated praise, following which she will persuade him to arouse the jealousy of the gods by walking into his home over precious fabrics (**3.4.1.4**); and although he realizes that her welcome has been immodest, Agamemnon lacks sufficient subtlety to hear its murderous intent.

1   Klytaimestra turns away from her husband after
    preventing him from leaving the chariot, and instead
    of greeting him, as she should, she starts by addressing
    the Elders. This beat is the prelude to her speech,
    setting up what she intends to do – to prove how
    much she loves her husband. She will return to this
    theme in beat 4, and again as she nears the climax in
    beats 6 to 7.

2 She describes emotionally the unbearable position of a woman left at home, prey to rumours.

3 She elaborates grotesquely on the accounts of Agamemnon's death that she alleges she has heard; in fact, she is glorying in the death that she is about to give him. Note especially: 'he'd have more holes in him than a net' (868); she herself will cast a net-like robe around Agamemnon to hold him down so she can penetrate his body three times with a sword. In beats 2 to 4 she exhibits a brazen hypocrisy that is breathtaking; and she treats the husband who is supposedly her lord and master as if he were just a specimen under examination ('this man here'; 860, 867).

4 She finishes the sequence of lies that began in beat 2 by even claiming that these rumours led her to attempt suicide.

5 Now for the tricky part. Klytaimestra must explain the absence of their son Orestes, so for the first time she addresses Agamemnon directly. Klytaimestra plays on any fears of insurrection that Agamemnon may have had. We (the Elders and the audience) know that he does have exactly such fears (845–50), but unless she was listening behind the doors,[29] she has no means of knowing that this is an argument that would appeal to her husband. But it does lull his fears; he makes no reference to Orestes in his reply. And with total hypocrisy she concludes: 'So this excuse of mine bears no deceit.' (886)

6 The sixth beat leads up to the peroration in beat 7. Once again, but from a completely new angle, Klytaimestra dwells on her supposed sufferings in her lonely bed while Agamemnon was away, painting a

---

[29]This is a real possibility. Klytaimestra has already shown an uncanny ability to enter at just the right moment in Scene 2, before 258, and especially in Scene 3, where she anticipates and blocks the Herald's movement towards entering the palace (587).

memorable but completely false picture. (In fact, she was having sex with Aigisthos.)

7   The climax of the speech, directed back to the Elders. Klytaimestra gathers together into one long sentence seven cliché metaphors for the joy created by Agamemnon's return, and at the climax does something deeply shocking to a Greek audience; she prostrates herself full-length at the king's feet. (We know this from Agamemnon's reply at 918–20: 'you must not/. . .as if I were an oriental king/gape grovelling on the ground to cry my praise.') It was a practice of Persian kings, loathed in the Athenian democracy, to demand this act of abasement from their subjects, and Klytaimestra here goes far beyond the bounds of Greek decorum.

8   Klytaimestra recovers from the outrageous climax of her homage, and calmly prays for the *daimōn* Jealousy to stand far away.

9   But then she immediately proceeds to ensure that Jealousy will be present here and now, and hostile to Agamemnon, by making him walk across fine robes that only the gods had the right to defile. She finally gives Agamemnon permission to enter the palace – but only by walking across them. And her last four lines (910–13) are full of ominous meaning; I shall return to that point and analyse the rest of the scene at **3.4.1.4**.

Dividing long speeches like this into beats, isolating the character's intent in each beat, and then building back to a coherent whole, will solve the problems that they may pose at first sight. And, of course, appropriate movements must be devised – in this case, an alternation between address to the Elders and to Agamemnon, and an alternation between stillness and movement.[30]

---

[30]For a complementary account of this speech, cf. Ley 2014: 20–5. For the blocking evolved in my production, cf. Ewans 1995: 142ff.

3.4.1.3 *Dialogue and three-actor scenes*

In Greek tragedy, dialogue is usually structured by the form known as *stichomythia* (literally, 'step-speech') – passages in which two actors exchange either single lines, or less frequently pairs of lines, or sometimes half-lines. It is as if the characters were linked by an invisible string, pulling each other in opposite directions until it snaps – as it does at line 523 in the example below. And occasionally there are three solo actors in the playing area, though such scenes are very carefully controlled by the playwright. A section that is a good example of both dialogue and a three-actor scene occurs in Sophocles' *Antigone*; the brothers Eteokles and Polyneikes have fought to the death, Eteokles defending the city of Thebes and Polyneikes leading a force attempting to invade it and take the throne from him. The new ruler, their uncle Kreon, decrees that Eteokles shall be buried with full honours, while the corpse of Polyneikes will be left on the battlefield to rot; anyone who attempts to bury him will suffer the penalty of death. Their sister Antigone refuses to accept the situation, and buries Polyneikes. She is captured doing so, and in a famous speech (450ff.) invokes the 'unwritten laws' of the gods as having more power than Kreon's mortal edict. Kreon reacts angrily, viewing Antigone's deed as an attack on his male pre-eminence: 'Truly I am the man no longer, she's the man/if she can win this victory without a punishment' (484–5). He also plans to execute Antigone's sister Ismene, whom he accuses (wrongly) of being complicit in the deed, and orders his Bodyguard to go inside and bring her out of the house. But this does not happen straight away.[31]

Antigone launches the dialogue with a short speech:

Antigone   Do you want to do more than kill me?
Kreon   No, that's all I want.

---

[31]This is an example of a confrontational *stichomythia*. The form can also be used in a less abrasive way, for example where one character wants to elicit information from another, and the latter is willing to give it. Cf. e.g. Euripides, *Iphigenia Among the Taurians*, 246ff.

Antigone   Then why do you delay? Nothing you say
  is pleasant to me, or would ever please me;   500
  and I'm sure you too hate every word of mine.
  What else could I have done which is
  more glorious than placing my dear brother
  in his grave? I know these men approve
  of what I've done; but fear has locked their tongues.   505
  Rulers have many privileges – one is that you can
  both do and say whatever you desire.

Kreon   You are the only Theban who sees things
  this way.

Antigone   These men see too; their mouths fawn on
  your will.

Kreon   D'you feel no shame if you feel differently?   510

Antigone   There is no shame in paying honour to your
  kin.

Kreon   The man who died opposing him; was he not
  kin as well?

Antigone   Yes, my mother's and my father's son.

Kreon   Then why pay honours he will see as impious?

Antigone   The dead man's corpse will not bear witness
  you are right.   515

Kreon   He will, because you give the same respect to
  him as to our enemy.

Antigone   It was his brother, not a slave who died.

Kreon   Trying to conquer this our land, while he
  defended it.

Antigone   I don't care; Haides wants these rites.

Kreon   A wicked man should not receive the same
  care as a good.   520

Antigone   Who knows if that's not right among the
  dead below?

Kreon   An enemy never deserves love, even when he's
  dead.

Antigone   I was not born to hate my relatives, but to give
  them my love.

Kreon   If you want to give love, go to the underworld

and love them there. No woman will rule over me while
    I'm alive.   525

Enter **Bodyguard** *from the* skēnē, *leading* **Ismene.**

1 Councillor   Ismene has been brought outside
    pouring out tears of love for her sister;
    a cloud of grief casts shades
    of sorrow over her flushed face
    and drenches her cheeks.   530
Kreon   You lurked snakelike inside the house
    and drank my life-blood secretly, so I was ignorant
    of nurturing two revolutionary, destructive girls.
    Now tell me; did you have a share
    in burying that man, or will you swear your
    innocence?   535
Ismene   I did the deed – if she will let me – and
    I want to take my share of blame.
Antigone   Justice will not allow you to do that, because
    you did not want to and I did not share my deed with
    you.
Ismene   But now you are in trouble, I am not
    ashamed   540
    to sail with you across this sea of suffering.
Antigone   Haides and those below know who buried him;
    I cannot love a friend who is a friend in words alone.
Ismene   My sister, please do not reject me; let me
    die with you, and pay due honour to the dead.   545
Antigone   You cannot share my death, and cannot claim
    work which you did not touch. My death will be
    enough.
Ismene   How could I want to live, if I lose you?
Antigone   Ask Kreon – you depend on him.
Ismene   Why do you taunt me? It will not help you.   550
Antigone   If I am mocking you, it hurts me too.
Ismene   What else could I now do to help?
Antigone   Save yourself. I won't be jealous if you can
    survive.

Ismene   I'm desperate. Will you not let me share your
   fate?
Antigone   No. You chose to live, while I chose death.   555
Ismene   I spoke; I tried to stop you.
Antigone   People up here approved of your ideas; the
   dead of mine.
Ismene   But now we are both equally condemned.
Antigone   Take courage. You are still alive – but my soul
   died
some time ago, so I could help the dead.   560
Kreon   I think that of these two girls one
   has just gone mad; the other always was.
Ismene   Yes, my lord; when people suffer they cannot
   always stay sane.
Kreon   You didn't, when you chose to join with her in
   wickedness.   565
Ismene   Why should I want to live alone, without her?
Kreon   This girl – don't speak of her. She is already
   dead.
Ismene   Will you kill her, engaged to your own son?
Kreon   Other women have furrows he can plough.
Ismene   No one was ever bound as close as him to
   her.   570
Kreon   I will not let my sons get worthless wives.
Ismene   Poor, dearest Haimon, how your father
   wrongs you![32]
Kreon   You and your bedroom talk are getting on my
   nerves.
Ismene   Will you take her away from your own son?
Kreon   For me, Haides will stop their wedding plans.   575

---

[32]One early edition attributed this line to Antigone. But nowhere else in the
play does she evidence any affection for Haimon, and the line plays best if
nothing interrupts the heated confrontation between Ismene and Kreon. It is
Ismene, not Antigone, who has been engaged in 'bedroom talk'. Cf. Griffith
1999: 217.

Ismene   So it is certain she must die?[33]
Kreon   On that we are agreed. (*To* **Bodyguard**.)
     No more delay; take her
   inside. From now on they must be
   just women, not allowed to roam at large.
   Even brave people try to run away, when they   580
   see Haides coming near to end their lives.

Kreon's statement that all he wants is Antigone's death is the 'launching-pad' for her strong nine-line response, which itself is the launching-pad for the following *stichomythia*. This is conducted in single lines, and you will note how at first each character picks up a word or words from the previous line to which to respond directly; e.g. 'You are the only Theban who *sees things* this way' > 'These men *see* too'; 'D'you feel *no shame*' > 'There is *no shame*'; 'The dead man's corpse *will not* bear witness' > 'He *will* (508–16). This close mode of statement and response then widens out during the remainder of the dialogue, which steadily becomes more intense – and should be played that way, gaining speed and volume – until Antigone's crowning statement: 'I was not born to hate my relatives, but to give them my love.' (523). On this line I chose in my production to have Antigone break away from direct confrontation with Kreon and address these words to the air and to the audience. Kreon was therefore forced to go after her and address his truly horrible closing lines to her back. Note that he has two lines after a sequence entirely in one-to-one; this marks that the first subsection of the scene is at an end.

Now Sophocles drives the scene to its climax by introducing the third actor in the character of Ismene. The vast majority of the original audience could not see her facial expression, so no attempt would have been made to portray it on the mask; a short intervention by one of the Councillors establishes the

---

[33]Some manuscripts ascribe this line to the choros of Councillors. But again, this interrupts the one-to-one interaction between Ismene and Kreon (at its climax!); much is lost and nothing is gained by this attribution.

essential facts that she is crying, and her face is flushed. Kreon leads off the next section by asking Ismene to confirm or deny her complicity with Antigone; but in a surprise move her response (two lines) is picked up not by Kreon but by Antigone, who engages her sister in a *stichomythia*, angry that Ismene now wants to share the responsibility for the burial. This *stichomythia* begins intensely – both sisters are emotional, and with very good reason; but when Antigone thinks she has won it ('my death will be enough', 547), Ismene surprisingly ups the ante, moving the argument from two-line to one-line exchange as she pours out her feelings; both sisters are now even more intense.

Once again, as with the first sequence between Antigone and Kreon, the end of the one-to-one exchange with Ismene is marked by a character, this time Antigone, speaking a pair of lines (559–60). At this point Kreon, who has stood aside during the sisters' argument, intervenes, commenting to the Councillors (or to his Bodyguard) that the two girls are insane. Now Ismene engages him in dialogue; note how at no point in the scene do all three characters interact, since as already noted (**1.5**) there might be difficulty for the ancient audience in making out who spoke which lines, especially with two actors currently playing young women. That difficulty does not apply in a modern mask-less production in a much smaller theatre with both male and female actors, but the scene still requires careful blocking. Ismene must pivot away from her sister (Antigone is silent for the remainder, probably facing out into the audience) to pick up Kreon's remark (which was about her and her sister, but not directed to her) and take the initiative in confronting him, forcing him to argue with her. Like Antigone in the first *stichomythia* of the scene, Ismene too is passionate and therefore her following dialogue with Kreon is in one-to-one format.

This time the closure is not achieved by giving a character two lines. Instead Kreon cruelly responds to Ismene's: 'So it is certain she must die?' with 'On that we are agreed' (756–7); he then turns to his Bodyguard, ordering him to take the two women to what he (together with most Athenian males) regards as their proper place – inside the house. His five lines close the scene.

The careful construction of this sub-scene, the alternation between short speeches, two-line and one-line *stichomythia*, makes it far more intense than if Sophocles had composed it in a free format. The combination of high emotion and strict formal control makes for a truly explosive piece of theatre.[34]

3.4.1.4 Props

In Greek tragedy (as opposed to comedy, see below **3.4.2.3**) props are rare, and often crucial when they are used. Graham Ley has studied the practical implications of five significant props in plays by Sophocles and Euripides;[35] I do not wish to go over ground that he has covered, so I shall return to the scene in Aeschylus where Agamemnon arrives back from conquering Troy, and consider Klytaimestra's use of the robes.[36] To continue from where we left off in **3.4.1.2**; maidservants have just strewn rich pieces of finely woven cloth, at Klytaimestra's command, between Agamemnon's chariot (almost certainly at the centre of the playing space) and the *skēnē* doors. This instantly and drastically changes the dynamic of the performance space, by adding an impressive visual feature; how will Agamemnon respond?

---

[34]To view my production of this scene, visit 'Sophocles' *Antigone* (1996 production)' on YouTube and scroll across to begin at 27:23. For comments on my blocking decisions cf. Ewans (ed.) 1999: 220–2.

[35]Ley 2014: 165–220. He analyses the use of Iphigenia's letter in Euripides' *Iphigenia Among the Taurians*, the cradle in Euripides' *Ion*, the children in Euripides' *Medea*, the dead child Astyanax on Hektor's shield in Euripides' *Trojan Women*, and the empty urn in Sophocles' *Elektra*. Cf. also Mueller 2015.

[36]This scene has been much discussed, but the only treatments from a theatrical point of view that I know of, except of course for my commentary (Ewans 1995: 142–7), are Taplin 1978: 78–83 and Ley 2007: 30–2.

Agamemnon Daughter of Leda, guardian of my house,
  you matched your speech quite closely to my
    absence;   915
  it was very long. And modest praise would be
  a gift I should receive from other mouths than yours.
  As for all this, you must not treat me softly
  like a woman, nor as if you were from oriental lands
  gape grovelling upon the ground to cry my praise. 920
  Nor should you make my path into the house
    subject to jealousy
  by strewing it with cloths: the gods alone deserve
    such honour;
  I, a mortal man, can't walk upon such beautiful
  and finely woven robes without evoking fear.
  I tell you, pay me the reverence due a man, and
    not a god.   925
  my fame shouts out aloud; it does not need the aid
  of beautiful foot-wiping cloths; and the gods'
    greatest gifts
  are sense and judgement. Count only that man
    fortunate
  who ends his life in peace and happiness.
  If I can always act in such a way, I can be
    confident.   930

Klytaimestra Now tell me this, and tell me what you
  judge to be the truth.

Agamemnon Know that I never will destroy my
  judgement.

Klytaimestra In a time of danger would you vow before
  the gods to do this thing?

Agamemnon Yes, if a prophet told me this is what
  I have to do.

Klytaimestra If Priam had achieved all you have,
  what would he have done?   935

Agamemnon I think he certainly would walk upon
  the robes.

Klytaimestra In that case do not fear the censure of
 mere men.
Agamemnon The people murmur, and their voice is
 full of strength.
Klytaimestra But no one can be praised who is not
 envied too.
Agamemnon All this desire for conflict is
 unwomanly.   940
Klytaimestra Yet for the prosperous even defeat
 shows grace.
Agamemnon So do you really value victory in this?
Klytaimestra Give way; you win if you have yielded
 of your own free will to me.
Agamemnon Well, if it is your wish, let someone
 quickly take
from me these boots, the gear that's subject to my
 feet;   945

A **Maidservant** *removes his boots.*

and as I walk upon these sea-dyed crimson garments
 of the gods,
may Jealousy not strike me from a distant eye.
I feel great awe as I destroy part of my house; my feet
ruin the wealth of this rich, silver-purchased web.

Agamemnon *steps from the chariot.*

Enough of that; as for this stranger,   950
welcome her into our house; the god looks kindly
 from afar
on those who conquer, but do not abuse their power.
No one wears the yoke of slavery with willingness;
and she has come back here with me, the flower
 chosen
by the army as my gift from all our wealth. 955
But since I've been subdued into obeying you in this,
I trample crimson as I go into my house.

> **Agamemnon** *moves to the edge of the robes,*
> *but then hesitates.*

Klytaimestra There is the sea, and who shall drain it dry?
  It breeds an ever-self-renewing stream
  of crimson dye for clothing, worth its weight in
    silver ore;   960
  thanks to the gods the house is rich in goods
  like these; my king, your house has never suffered
    poverty.
  I would have vowed the trampling down of many
    vestments, if
  we had been told in oracles it was
  the only way to bring this man back here alive;
  for when the root is there, the leafage comes over
    a house   965
  extending shade above to shield us from the dog-star
    heat;
  now you have come back to your house and home,
  that signals warmth has come back in the winter-time;
  and when Zeus makes the wine from bitter, unripe
    grapes   970
  then there is coolness in the house
  when he, the man, fulfils his role and roams around
    his halls.

> *Exit* **Agamemnon** *over the robes into the* skēnē.
> *The* **Maidservants** *remove the robes and exeunt*
> *into the* skēnē.

Zeus, Zeus fulfiller; now fulfil my prayer;
take care to fulfil all of this that you intend.

> *Exit* **Klytaimestra** *into the* skēnē. *Doors close.*

The robes have both a literal and a symbolic meaning. Literally, they are finely woven, expensive dyed fabrics ('this rich, silver-purchased web', 949); to defile such things is a privilege of the gods, as Agamemnon rightly says at 922–5; and for him to usurp their role in such a way is to invite their jealousy. That of course is Klytaimestra's aim in this scene. Meanwhile there is symbolic meaning; the colour of the woven robes is the colour of dried blood. This evokes the sacrifice of Iphigenia, which Klytaimestra will avenge by killing Agamemnon (1411ff., 1432);[37] it also evokes the disproportionally many lives (436ff.) lost in the ten-year siege of Troy 'for a [wanton] woman's sake' – a motif that the Elders introduced into the first half of the play at 63 and 448, and which is spoken by Agamemnon, startlingly without apparent irony, at 823.

So Klytaimestra's introduction of the robes raises the stakes of the scene to a lethal level. The issues are clearly stated in Agamemnon's reply. He is infuriated by the length of her speech, the fact that she, a woman, made it at all, and the complete abasement before him 'as if I were an oriental king' (918). Then he speaks about the robes, and rejects them completely as dangerous; to tread on them would be to lose 'sense and judgement' (928). And yet in just fifteen lines, Klytaimestra persuades him to do just this. How?

In the *stichomythia*, Agamemnon's replies to her arguments are weak and inadequate. I comment below in italics:

> **Klytaimestra** Now tell me this, and tell me what you
>   judge to be the truth.
> **Agamemnon** Know that I never will destroy my
>   judgement.

So far so good.

> **Klytaimestra** In a time of danger would you vow before
>   the gods to do this thing?

---

[37]In Katie Mitchell's 1999 National Theatre of Great Britain production, the robes were a collage of bloodstained little girls' dresses, over-emphasizing this point at the expense of removing the important image of the robes as priceless fabrics – but some audience members were understandably moved by it. Mitchell has subsequently admitted (2009: 3) that she concentrated on Iphigenia (who appeared as a silent ghost in some scenes in her production) at the expense of a balanced interpretation of the trilogy as a whole.

Agamemnon   Yes, if a prophet told me this is what
I have to do.

*But in this case, there has been no such instruction from
a seer.*

Klytaimestra   If Priam had achieved all you have,
what would he have done?   935
Agamemnon   I think he certainly would walk upon
the robes.

*But Priam was an oriental king (cf. 919) and Agamemnon, as
a Greek constitutional monarch, should certainly not follow
his example.*

Klytaimestra   In that case do not fear the censure of
mere men.
Agamemnon   The people murmur, and their voice is
full of strength.

*So it should not be ignored by usurping the privileges of the
gods. The response is half-hearted and procrastinating.*

Klytaimestra   But no one can be praised who is not
envied too.

*A brilliant reply, capitalizing on Agamemnon's weak previous
line.*

Agamemnon   All this desire for conflict is
unwomanly.   940

*Too late, Agamemnon realizes that his wife has been
arguing with him as if she were his equal, or indeed his
superior.*

Klytaimestra   Yet for the prosperous even defeat
shows grace.
Agamemnon   So do you really value victory in this?

*He fails to see that in the present situation her last line is
completely specious – and dangerous.*

Klytaimestra   Give way; you win if you have yielded of
      your own free will to me.

This too is sophistic; but it works.

Agamemnon   Well, if it is your wish, let someone
      quickly take
   From me these boots.   945

So, we near the climax; but Aeschylus will not let the audience
fail to understand the full significance of the robes. Agamemnon,
now that he has agreed to do the very thing that he earlier
stated would incur the jealousy of the gods, *hopes* that he will
not (946–9). He then outrages Klytaimestra even more, by
introducing his concubine, the army's gift to him, Kassandra
(though he does not name her). Klytaimestra will slaughter her
too. And Agamemnon ends by emphasizing that he has been
subdued by Klytaimestra into 'trampling' on the crimson
cloths.[38]

   Klytaimestra now launches into an extraordinary, highly
rhetorical speech, in which she compares the riches of their
house to those of the sea, states that she 'would have vowed
the trampling down of many vestments/if we had been told in
oracles it was/the only way to bring this man back here alive'
(932–4), and ends with a paean to this moment when the man
has returned to his house. Agamemnon could perhaps be
treading over the robes during this speech; but it is too long for
that, even in the Greek playing space where there would
perhaps have been ten metres between the chariot at C and the

---

[38]This image has already been introduced, by the Elders in Choros 2: 'Once
someone said/the gods don't think it worth their while/to be concerned with
men who trample on/the beauty of a sacred thing; but he was impious' (369ff.).
Directors of Aeschylus need to be aware of the patterns of such recurrent
imagery in his tragedies, especially in the three dramas of the *Oresteia*. Though
not entirely satisfactory (*Eumenides* is not studied properly), Lebeck 1971 is
the fundamental study of the trilogy's imagery.

skēnē doors. Nor is there any motivation for him to start walking half-way through the speech. And clearly, he must not go in before hearing 967–72.

The solution that we arrived at in my production is reflected in the stage directions printed above. Like Karolos Koun later on, I chose to see Agamemnon as not proceeding, as he says he will at 956–7, but hesitating at the brink.[39] Klytaimestra's last speech is then a final act of persuasion; she needs to summon the immense strength of her will for one last time. Agamemnon then walks over the robes, the Maidservants remove them and Klytaimestra is left alone with the Elders for her passionate appeal to Zeus to fulfil her prayers. (He will.) Then she too goes into the palace. The Elders are deeply concerned about what they have seen, and express that concern in Choros 4, which follows.

3.4.1.5 Conclusion

I hope that this exploration of a speech, a dialogue sequence and the reactions needed for the deployment of a prop, helps you when you approach directing or acting a solo part in a Greek tragedy. The first thing to do when about to rehearse a scene is of course to establish the dramatic situation at that stage of the play, but once that is agreed in the rehearsal room, the next task is to break the scene down into sections and attend to the 'clues to action', which are, as we have seen in these examples, there to be found in the scripts. I am not saying that every detail of blocking, movement and gesture is implicit in the texts – far from it; but I *am* saying that these plays need and deserve careful thought about the characters' *aims* in every word they utter, due attention to the *form* in which the playwright has composed each scene and sub-scene, and a response to any scene that involves *props* that yield conclusions about when, how and above all why they are deployed. If this

---

[39]On Koun's National Theatre of Greece production cf. below pp. 184–6.

has been done, the movements and gestures, and modes of delivery of the text that are needed to make the play live in performance will emerge naturally, and can then be refined and elaborated during the rehearsal process.

3.4.2 Comedy

There is much to discover in a good translation of a comedy by Aristophanes; indeed, there is so much implicit in the script that there is almost no need to interpolate extra stage business to bring these comedies alive for a modern audience.[40] We will first examine as a case study the lead role in *The Women's Festival*, to elicit the comic techniques needed to realize it; then we will analyse a sequence from *Frogs*, to show how a *lazzo* full of comic business can be developed by close attention to the text. Finally, we will examine the use of props; comedy, unlike tragedy, uses many.

3.4.2.1 *The In-Law in* The Women's Festival

The role of Euripides' elderly In-Law in *The Women's Festival* is one of the most demanding, in terms of the acting techniques required, in the surviving comedies. Among other skills, he is required to be a gag man, perform slapstick, sustain a semi-plausible impersonation of a woman, and deliver parodies of female tragic dialogue and lyric. It must be a virtuoso performance.

In Scene 1 the In-Law begins as a typical Aristophanic, grumbling 'man in the street'; but he rapidly becomes the gag man to three 'straight' characters, Aristophanes' caricatures of the tragic playwrights Euripides and Agathon, and Agathon's Servant who comes out to announce that Agathon is about to compose tragic lyrics. For example:

---

[40]Cf. the Theatrical Commentaries on six Aristophanic comedies in Ewans 2010 and 2011.

> (**Servant**)   He's bending new planks made of words,
>   planing some and gluing others,
>   forging ideas, inventing metaphors, and melting   55
>   wax; he rounds the words to shape,
>   then casts them in the mould –
> **In-Law**   and sucks some cocks.
> **Servant**   What vulgar peasant has approached these
>   halls?
> **In-Law**   A man who's ready to take you and Agathon,
>   creator
>   of fine words, turn you around, bend you,   60
>   and bugger you with this prick!

Euripides is visiting the effeminate younger poet Agathon to implore him to go to the Women's Festival that very day, disguised as a woman, to speak up for him; he has heard that the women are conspiring to destroy him 'because I slander women in my tragedies' (85). Agathon comes out on the *ekkuklēma*, dressed very convincingly as a woman, and sings an antiphonal song between a priestess and her maidens (the first of many parodies of tragedy in the play). The In-Law responds to this with a trenchant speech (130ff.), querying – with good reason – which gender Agathon belongs to. The playwright explains that he is wearing female costume because he has to get into the character he is trying to create, and the In-Law, once again the gag man, ripostes: 'You must ride men on top, when you write about Phaidra' (154). The by-play continues until Euripides interrupts to make his request, which Agathon refuses for the good reason that if discovered by the women he would suffer an even worse fate than Euripides, because: 'I copy all the things they do/at night, and steal their natural rights as females' (205–6).

This moves the play on into a slapstick scene. The In-Law abruptly and implausibly offers to do what Agathon refused to do, and instantly Euripides asks him to strip off (to a body-stocking with a large artificial penis attached to it), borrows a razor and a torch from Agathon, shaves off the In-Law's beard and singes his private parts. Then Euripides borrows a dress, a wig, a belt and a scarf from Agathon so that the ludicrous impersonation of a woman by this elderly man can begin. Aristophanes then sets up the closing scenes of the play; the In-Law makes Euripides swear by all the gods to rescue him if he is discovered (269ff.).

Agathon has been wheeled back into the *skēnē*, and Euripides leaves. Now the In-Law must begin his impersonation; while the choros of Women and three solo women approach for the second day of the festival he adopts a female voice, in which (s)he addresses an imaginary slave, and offers up prayers to two leading female deities, Demeter and Persephone, for his own survival that day and for the well-being of 'her' children Pussy and Prickie (280ff.).

The Assembly of the Women begins – a parody of male assemblies – and the Women implement their resolve to discuss 'what we should do/ to make Euripides suffer, since we all think/he's done wrong' (377–9). Two women – Mika and a Garland Seller – make speeches, one long and one short, denouncing Euripides, and then the In-Law receives the speaker's garland and begins his speech in defence of Euripides (466ff.), arguing that women do all sorts of other wicked things that Euripides *hasn't* mentioned in his tragedies. It is extensive, brilliantly written, and rich in accounts of action that call out for mime – especially when 'she' describes how her lover fucked her 'head down/beside the altar of Apollo' (488–9). It also requires vocal impersonation of a woman and of her husband (here the actor can lapse back momentarily into his natural male voice), and of the croaking voice of the old crone at 514ff. These vocal impersonations need of course to be backed up by appropriate physical postures and gestures.

Naturally, this arouses the anger of the Women, but the In-Law, instead of mollifying them, incites them further by recounting even more 'things we do that Euripides never mentioned', in a free *stichomythia* argument with Mika, who at the end is threatening to pull out all of the In-Law's pubic hair.[41]

However, Aristophanes interrupts this climax that he does not want – a girlie fight – to proceed to the even funnier climax that he is aiming for. Kleisthenes, Athens' most notorious passive homosexual, appears in drag to tell the Women that Euripides has sent an old man, a relative of his, to spy on them disguised as a woman. In response, Kritylla, the leader of the women, asks Kleisthenes to interrogate them one by one to find out the imposter's identity. The In-Law buys time; he excuses himself for a moment to head into the mouth of the right *eisodos*, claiming that he needs to pee – but when he returns and is questioned about the secret rites of the festival, he fails to come up with enough correct answers. Kritylla demands that he strip off – and when his torso is revealed, there are naturally no breasts. Now follows a piece of literal slapstick, demanding virtuoso timing from the actor playing the In-Law; after fully divesting himself of his dress, he hides his penis by first pushing it to the back of his body, then to the front and then back again as Kleisthenes and Kritylla circle around him; but finally they spot it and the punch-line is, in my translation, 'What's this? A game of high-speed *shuttlecock*?' (648).[42]

The In-Law resumes his female costume, but suddenly seizes Mika's baby from her servant Mania, and rushes to the central altar, where he threatens it with the sacrificial knife. This action begins a parody of Euripides' tragedy *Telephos*, in which the

---

[41]*Stichomythia* in comedy can be much freer than the more formal one-to-one or two-to-two line exchanges that are the norm in tragedy (for which see **3.4.1.3**). Half-line exchanges do appear in later fifth-century tragedies, but the divisions into thirds and even quarters found in Aristophanes do not, except in the most agitated dialogues (e.g., Sophocles *Elektra* Choros 3, 823ff. and Euripides *Orestes* 1525).

[42]Aristophanes' original reference was to the shuttle service for goods across the Isthmus of Corinth. I have taken a liberty, and used an English pun, to make the effective meaning (above, **3.1.3**) available to a modern audience.

title figure seized Agamemnon's baby son Orestes and fled to an altar, threatening to kill the child unless the Greek chieftains gave him sanctuary. The actor must deliver a parody of a tragic character – until the In-Law unwraps the 'baby' and discovers that it is a full wineskin (733)! When Mika realizes that she has been found out, she continues to plead as if the wineskin were a real baby, and the In-Law continues to threaten to cut its throat if they attempt to drive him from the altar; then he actually does so, allowing Mika to catch some of 'her daughter's blood' in a bowl but spraying her with the rest of it. The comic effect of the last section of this scene is derived from the tension between the In-Law's discovery and the lines that Mika delivers as if the 'baby' was a real one.

The In-Law, marooned on the altar, resolves to try to send a message to Euripides, and introduces the theme that will dominate in the second part of the play; parodies of Euripidean rescue techniques. He remembers that in *Palamedes*, Oiax sent messages on oar-blades thrown into the sea; but he doesn't have any oar-blades, so he uses some votive tablets that are conveniently to hand beside the altar. But he has trouble carving them, and simply throws them in all directions. Not surprisingly, they do not reach Euripides.

The pace has been hectic for the last few sections of Scene 3; Aristophanes accordingly gives the lead actor and the audience some 'time out' as the choros perform their address to the audience, the *parabasis* (**3.5.3.2**) – in this play, naturally enough, a complaint about the mistreatment of women and a statement of their superiority to men.

The second part of *The Women's Festival* begins with an extended parody. The In-Law resolves to be 'Helen' from Euripides' tragedy of the previous year; so he must not only impersonate a woman taking refuge at a tomb, but also (mis-) perform actual tragic dialogue – together with some parodic comic insertions. Kritylla is now obliged to play the straight role, insisting on the reality of the situation against the bizarre acting-out of scenes involving Helen in Egypt, with Euripides coming to the rescue disguised as her husband Menelaos, in rags and covered with seaweed after having been wrecked on the shore. They play out Euripides' recognition scene, with an erotic twist; Helen's line 'At last you're here; come, come into your wife's arms' has changed to 'come into your wife's warm pussy' (912).

But the rescue attempt fails; an Executive from the Council arrives, summoned earlier by Mika, together with a Policeman; Euripides make a hasty retreat, promising to return. The Policeman leads the In-Law into the *skēnē*, under orders to bind him on a plank. This happens during the next Choros. The In-Law is then brought out on the *ekkuklēma*, bound to the plank, and the Policeman fetches a mat to lie on and goes to sleep.

Re-enter Euripides, now on the *mēchanē* disguised as Perseus. He makes an overflight but fails to land; nonetheless the In-Law recognizes that he must play Andromeda, bound to a rock and at the mercy of a savage sea-monster until Perseus rescues her. This prompts the most virtuoso performance in the play; the In-Law sings a lyric monody as Andromeda, while also lapsing frequently into reflections on the reality of his own pitiable position – singing all the while, presumably in a high voice for the real lines from *Andromeda* (a play which, like *Helen*, had been performed only the previous year, so it would be fresh in the minds of the audience) and in a low voice for the lines sung as the In-Law.[43] A comic sub-scene follows in which Andromeda is joined by Echo (apparently this happened in Euripides' actual, now lost drama), who exasperates first the In-Law – still attempting to sing as Andromeda – and then the Policeman by repeating their lines. After this, Euripides reappears on the *mēchanē*, and makes a perfect landing. But the impersonation fails; when 'Perseus' declares his love for 'Andromeda', the Policeman shows him the In-Law's prick, and when Euripides commits himself to freeing 'her' from her chains, the Policeman drives him away with his whip.

---

[43]In my translation I mark lines throughout the song A for Andromeda and I for the In-Law, to help the actor. Ewans 2010: 148–9.

The Andromeda parody monody was the In-Law's high spot in the second half of the play. His part from now on is relatively minor. Euripides returns on foot and makes a deal with the Women; if he can have his relative back, he won't tell their husbands, on their return from the war, what they have got up to. The Women agree at once; Euripides, now disguised as an old woman, gets a dancing girl, Fawn, to seduce the Policeman; then while they are having sex inside the *skēnē*, Euripides frees the In-Law, who promptly runs home. The Women misdirect the Policeman, when he comes out, into pursuing them out the wrong *eisodos*, and then bring the play to a close.

This case study has shown the virtuosity that Aristophanes could demand from his lead actor; in particular he has to act as gag man or straight; to participate in slapstick scenes; to impersonate a woman as convincingly as his character can, and to speak and sing parodies of tragedy.[44]

3.4.2.2 *A* lazzo *in* Frogs

In *Frogs*, Dionysos, caricatured as a pot-bellied glutton and coward wearing a saffron dress and slippers, embarks on a journey to the underworld to fetch back his favourite tragedian, Euripides (who had died in the year before this comedy was performed). He is accompanied by his slave Xanthias, and the two lead actors play a brilliant comedy double act, each alternating between gag man and straight man for 674 lines, before Xanthias is written out so that the actor can play one of the tragedians Aeschylus and Euripides during the competition in Haides that occupies much of the second half of the play (see further **3.4.2.3**).

Dionysos looks ludicrous. He is wearing a lionskin over his lounging costume and carries a club; he hopes to penetrate

---

[44]In my performances (a full production, except that scripts were in hand), the student actor Mark Coles made a very effective stab at a role that really demands a much older professional. Search YouTube under 'Aristophanes' The Women's Festival (2006 production)'.

Haides in disguise as Herakles, who once went down there to capture the dog Kerberos. On their way to Haides, Dionysos visits Herakles himself for advice, attempts without success to hire a Corpse to carry their luggage, and finally arrives at the shore of a bottomless lake, where he pays Charon, the ferryman of the dead, to convey him across. Being a slave, Xanthias must go round on land, and during the scene in the boat where Dionysos encounters the Frogs and has a lyric contest with them, the actor playing Xanthias probably walked around the perimeter of the *orchēstra* wearily, carrying their baggage.

The scene that we are going to examine begins when Dionysos has paid off Charon and got out of the boat. It is a remarkable scene, as although there are no props involved, realization of the dialogue demands considerable physicalization by the two actors. Here it is, with my suggestions for movement in the original stage shape in italics (though this blocking would work almost as well in a proscenium arch production). This set of movements was developed over several workshops.

> **Dionysos** (*disembarking from Charon's boat, which stagehands pull off by the right* eisodos, *and tiptoeing blindly and cautiously through the 'darkness' of Haides – around EBR.*)
> Xanthias! Where's Xanthias? Oh Xanthias!   271
>
> > **Xanthias** *calls back from where he completed his circuit of the* orchēstra, *possibly ECR.*

> **Xanthias**   Cooee!
> **Dionysos**   Come here!

Miming movement in total darkness, as if neither of them is able to see, they grope their way forward toward each other's voice and bump into each other.

> **Xanthias** (*recovering from the collision*)   Welcome, master.
> **Dionysos**   What did you find on your way?

Xanthias (*miming the difficulties of walking blindly
    through mud*)
                                        Darkness and mud.
Dionysos   Did you see anywhere those father-beaters
    and perjurers he told us about?

Both characters now act as people able to see perfectly.

Xanthias (*drawing D to C/ FC and indicating the
    audience with a large gesture*)
                                        Don't you?
Dionysos (*his face surveying the central sector of the
    audience*)
    Yes, by Poseidon, and I can still see them.   275

Beat. Then turning to X.

    What will we do next?
Xanthias   We'd better get out of here.

Moves a few paces towards the L eisodos.

    This is the place where that fellow said
    we'd find wild beasts.
Dionysos   He'll be sorry he said that.

*He starts to move, and his movements become more
expansive as he delivers this speech, striding in an arc around
part of the front half of the playing space to indicate his
increasing overconfidence.*[45]

    He was just telling lies to scare me   280
    out of sheer jealousy because I am so brave.
    There's no one as conceited as that Herakles.
    Myself, I rather hoped we would encounter one
    and do a deed that's worthy of our noble quest.

---

[45]Remember that the front half of the *orchēstra* is a weaker position than the
rear half.

Xanthias (*who has moved to C to observe D's vainglorious
      manner more closely, heartily agrees*)   Absolutely!
(*Then with a total change of tone.*)
            But listen, I can hear a sound.   285
Dionysos   Where is it?
Xanthias   Behind us (*i.e. at the rear of the* orchēstra.)
Dionysos (*races to X and makes him stand between
      himself and the source of the sound*)
                              Go behind.
Xanthias   Now it's in front. (*Pointing forward towards
      EFL.*)[46]
Dionysos (*forcing X to reverse their positions so X is
      nearer to EFL than he is*)
                  You go in front.
Xanthias (*retreating slightly from C towards BR*)   By
      Zeus, I see a gigantic monster.
Dionysos (*cowering behind X and retreating even
      more toward EBR*)
   What's it like?
Xanthias (*peering towards EFL*)   Terrible! It is all
      kinds of shapes;
      Now it's a cow, now it's a mule, and now . . .
      (*Moving towards EFL.*)
   it's a beautiful girl.   290
Dionysos (*pushes X aside and races to FL*)   Where is
      she? Let me at her.
Xanthias   No! It's not a girl any more; now it's a dog.
Dionysos (*stops instantly, turns, and runs back behind
      X towards BR*)
   It must be the Empousa.

---

[46]It could just as well be EFR, so this choice is arbitrary to that extent. But the
Empousa cannot be imagined as being in the rear half of the *orchēstra*, or the
actors will be facing away from too much of the audience at once in the
following business; and it cannot be EFC, as this would pre-empt Dionysos'
desperate run for safety to his priest at the end of the sequence.

Xanthias   (*perhaps stepping slightly forward
    towards EFL to 'see more clearly'*)
                                        Yes, her whole face
    is shining like a fire.
Dionysos (*still cowering BR*)   And has she got a
    copper leg?
Xanthias   Yes by Poseidon; and the other one is made
    of donkey dung.   295
Dionysos (*turns away from X, to address the R side of
    the audience, and makes a gesture of despair*)
    Where can I go?
Xanthias (*turns away from D, to address the other [L]
    side of the audience, and copies D's gesture*)   And
    me?
Dionysos (*rushes to EFC, to the centre front row of
    the audience where the VIPs sit, kneels, and begs*)
    My priest, please save me; let me drink with you
    after the show.

In this scene virtuoso acting is required. The actors begin by miming in total darkness; then suddenly this convention is abandoned, and they can see everything perfectly – including the audience, who are the victims of a gag (274–6). Then Dionysos forgets his real character so far as to wish for an adventure 'worthy of our noble quest' (284) – and this gives Xanthias the idea of showing what an utter coward his master actually is, by pretending to see a shape-shifting monster, the Empousa. The following sequence plays itself if Xanthias stays mostly near C, manipulating Dionysos like a puppet on a string, as he imagines the monster first behind them, then in front (provoking Dionysos to rapid, panic-stricken running to take shelter between Xanthias and the supposed position of the Empousa), then as various animals, then as a beautiful girl. Since Dionysos in this play is characterized as a ladies' man,[47] this prompts him to charge towards the apparition – but Xanthias once

---

[47]738–40: 'SLAVE He's a gentleman, /Your master. XANTHIAS How could he not be? /He can only do two things, drinking and fucking.'

again declares that it has changed shape, prompting an equally rapid retreat by Dionysos. Xanthias' ensuing descriptions make Dionysos more and more terrified, until he steps out of the play by supplicating his Priest (in the centre of the front row) to save him – and for *Frogs* to win the prize, as the Priest only entertained the winning production team after the performances.

It will be seen that this scene demands great physicality, especially from the actor playing Dionysos; it will also be seen that all the necessary business is implied by and generated from the spoken words.

3.4.2.3 Props

Tragedy makes rare but highly meaningful use of props (above, **3.4.1.4**); by contrast, Aristophanic comedy is rich in properties.[48] They are used in two main ways; by accumulation, to build up gradually to a crucial scene; and by introduction at the climax of a scene that before that has proceeded with speech and song alone.

Accumulated props

As an example of accumulation, we will look at the build-up to the 'chopping-block speech' in *Acharnians*. Dikaiopolis is an honest, Athenian citizen from the countryside; his name means 'Just City'. He delivers this speech in an attempt to convince the most militant Athenians, the men from the village of Acharnai who form the choros, that the Athenians are at least as responsible as the Spartans for the outbreak of the Peloponnesian War. He is terrified of them, and resolves:

> So now, before I speak, let me put on some gear
> to make me look completely pitiful.

(383–4)

---

[48]Lists of the props needed are given following the cast lists for the six plays translated in Ewans (ed.) 2010 and 2011.

And to get it he goes to – Euripides! The great man is at work, and reluctant to come out, but finally consents to be wheeled out on the *ekkuklēma*. He is on a chaise longue, dressed in a beggar's costume and surrounded by small props. Also, on the *ekkuklēma* is a rack of tragic costumes, mostly beggar's rags. (Here, as later with Agathon in *The Women's Festival* [3.4.2.1], Aristophanes supposes for comic effect that the tragic poets needed to get into costume in order to write parts for their characters.) Dikaiopolis first seeks out the meanest, most beggarly costume in the collection, which turns out to be that of Telephos, and then starts begging for props; Telephos' felt cap, a walking stick, a little basket ('I do not really need it; I'd just like to have one', 455), a little cup with a chip in its lip, a little jar plugged with a sponge – Euripides, increasingly exasperated, replies: 'You bastard, I am losing all my tragedies' (463) – and just one thing more; some withered leaves to line his basket. Euripides responds: 'You are destroying me; my plays are gone' (470).

But then comes the punch line; Dikaiopolis is about to leave, when he realizes that he has forgotten to ask for some chervil (Aristophanes here as later in *Frogs* [840] makes fun of the fact that Euripides' mother, as Dikaiopolis points out, ran a vegetable shop). This is too much; Euripides refuses, ands retreats into the house on the *ekkuklēma*. 'Dear heart, I've got to go without the chervil' says Dikaiopolis (480); but nonetheless, armed with his Telephos costume and his collection of props, he advances to the chopping block on which he had undertaken to give his speech, and makes an eloquent case – part comic and part serious – that the Athenians were as much to blame for starting the war as their opponents (498ff.). It is a remarkable performance, the more so because Dikaiopolis has assumed the character of a beggar through the costume and props that he has borrowed from Euripides. And he is echoing and parodying the situation of Telephos in Euripides' tragedy, who gave a speech on the chopping block in defence of his Mysians' right to fight back against the Greek invaders. He also speaks as if he were the comic poet, defending himself in this speech against slanders by Kleon, a leading politician.[49] The speech is so effective that it splits the choros; half of the Acharnians are incensed, but half are converted. (Later they will all side with Dikaiopolis as he pursues his private peace with Sparta and her allies.) But its effect would be greatly diminished if it had not been for the preceding scene, in which Dikaiopolis solicited ever more (and ever more ludicrous) props from Euripides to give him the courage to make the speech.

A prop introduced at the climax of a scene

The last part of *Frogs* is a competition in Haides between Aeschylus and Euripides, each seeking to be taken back to Athens by Dionysos to save the city (which, at the time of performance, was in dire straits). 'Aeschylus' is represented as a stalwart of the 'good old days', the victories of Marathon and Salamis; 'Euripides' as a representative of all that is slick, modern and immoral. (Both are, naturally in Aristophanes, exaggerated caricatures.) The contest begins with verbal abuse, then issues of morality take over; after that Euripides critiques Aeschylus' prologues, and Aeschylus demolishes Euripides' own prologues by interrupting with the absurd half-line 'lost his flask of oil' two or three lines into his recital of each of them. Then the contest escalates to song and dance; Euripides parodies Aeschylean lyrics, and Aeschylus in turn first parodies Euripides' lyrics, then sings a brilliant send-up of a Euripidean monody.

So far the contest has been entirely verbal and then musical; but to bring it to a climax, Aristophanes introduces a prop, a large pair of scales into which each poet is to speak a line of verse (1377ff.). Aeschylus wins decisively, with lines

---

[49]Most scholars assume that this section is spoken as Aristophanes, but Bowie 1988 presents arguments for the aggrieved poet being Eupolis.

containing far greater weight than those of Euripides, and then declares:

> Stop going verse for verse; let him
> get in the scales himself, his children, wife, Kephisophon,
> and sit with all his books –
> and I'll recite just two of my own verses.

(1407FF.)

Dionysos still cannot decide and seeks specific political advice; but the contest has been brought to a convincing end by the sophisticated development from verbal abuse and moral considerations to delivery of parodied verses, first dialogue and then lyric, up to the point where the comic prop, the pair of scales, is introduced to bring the competition to its climax.

3.4.2.4 Conclusion

As with tragedy, comedy requires close concentration on the script. Characters may react in ways and do things that are completely bizarre, as each Aristophanic comedy inhabits its own fantasy world; but actors, especially those with lead roles, need to be attuned to the many different modes of acting that these scripts require from them. As we saw from our case study of the In-Law, a wide variety of techniques are necessary for realizing the text – and the same applies to other lead characters, such as Dikaiopolis, Paphlagon in *Knights,* Lysistrata and Dionysos in *Frogs.* Smaller parts tend to call for a lesser variety of acting techniques, but can still make considerable demands (cf. e.g. Myrrhine in *Lysistrata*). And a fine sense of comic timing is essential.

Verbal *lazzi* implying much physical movement are also a feature of these scripts; our example from *Frogs* in **3.4.2.2** could be paralleled for example with the hamper scene in *Knights* (Scene 4, 1151 ff.) or the seduction of Kinesias by Myrrhine (*Lysistrata* Scene 5, 870ff.). Both of these scenes are also good examples of the additive use of props leading to a climax, which we analysed in detail with Dikaiopolis' visit to Euripides in *Acharnians*.[50]

3.5 The Choros

3.5.1 Introduction

In my first two productions, Aeschylus' *Libation Bearers* (1983) and *Eumenides* (1985), I asked a composer to set parts – but not the whole – of the choral odes to sung music. It was not disastrous, but neither was it satisfactory, since it slowed the pace of the action, to my mind unacceptably (though the Finale of *Eumenides*, a place where a mood of solemn but joyful ceremony is called for, was effective). I abandoned this practice when directing *Agamemnon* (1986), and adopted what has been my preference ever since for both tragedy and comedy; to have the choroses choreographed (of course), accompanied by instrumental or electronic music, and with each stanza normally spoken by an individual member of the choros, emphasized rarely where appropriate by a unison declamation. This ensures that the words of the text are audible; and since in the original productions they had precedence over the music (unlike the case in many operas), this is a very important consideration.

There is no reason to suppose that ancient choroses sung the whole of the lyrics in unison; some sections were obviously divided, as in Aeschylus *Agamemnon* 474ff., and *Eumenides*

---

[50]Later in *Acharnians* (1097ff.) there is an almost unperformable sequence where the belligerent general Lamachos orders his servant to bring out one by one the things that he needs to go out to battle, while in one-to-one *stichomythia* with him, Dikaiopolis orders *his* servant to bring out what he needs for a feast. To fulfil the implications of the script, this would have to be performed at breakneck speed, perhaps with the servants running and dropping properties as they rush in and out of the *skēnē* doors as they attempt to fulfil the impossible number of orders. Cf. Ewans 2011: 220–1.

Choroses 1 and 2, where the Furies enter individually and clearly those not yet in the playing space can't sing (Ewans 1995: xxiv–xxv). And many other choral lyrics would have benefitted from individuals singing separate stanzas or parts of stanzas.[51]

In some productions, choral lyrics are abandoned altogether. David Rudkin's otherwise fine 1978 'version' of *Hippolytos* reduced the choros to one speaking character (in the first scene a Man of the Household, and then in the remainder of the play a Young Woman). This upset the balance of the original texts between lyrics and dialogue; the whole drama became spoken by individuals, as if it were just like a modern play of Rudkin's own – though there was some instrumental music from one musician. Rudkin was unapologetic; 'Euripides' audience weren't watching a "Greek" play. They were watching a play of their own. So must we be.'[52] And he has a point.

Peter Hall went to the opposite extreme; his 1981 *Oresteia* was very frequently punctuated by an abrasive score composed by Harrison Birtwistle, including in dialogue scenes. This too upset the careful balance of the Greek text. I believe that music should only be used in passages that were lyrics in the original. Lines that were originally chanted or sung can easily be spotted in a good translation, as they are much shorter than the dialogue lines; in my published versions all such lines are double-indented.

3.5.2 Tragedy

3.5.2.1 A choral ode

In Sophocles' *Antigone,* immediately after the scene analysed in **3.4.1.3,** the Bodyguard pushes the sisters indoors to await

---

[51]Cf. Alexander-Lillicrap 2022, Commentary on Euripides' *Iphigenia among the Taurians* 216–17, 221–2 for workshopped examples.
[52]Rudkin 1980: iii.

their fate and Kreon remains outside. The Councillors then perform the following lyrics:

CHOROS 3

Councillors
> (**A1**) Blessed are all who live without tasting misfortune.
> When a house is shaken by the gods, disaster
> never stops – creeping across the generations,   585
> like the surge of the salt sea
> driven by fierce winds from Thrakia
> across the darkness of the deep;
> it churns the black sand from the depths,   590
> and headlands, struck by bitter winds,
> cry out and groan.

> (**A2**) From long ago I've seen that in our royal house
> new sorrows fall upon the sorrows of the dead;   595
> no generation frees the next, but some god
> strikes them down, and there is no escape.
> In Oidipous' house the light was scattered
> faintly above the last roots of the family;   600
> but now the bloody knife
> of the gods of the underworld
> cuts it away with crazy speech
> and Furies in the mind.

> (**B1**) What human outrage, Zeus,
> could ever check your power? –   605
> the power which neither all-ensnaring Sleep
> nor the years' unrelenting months
> can overcome; Time does not age you,
> but you are the lord of all
> Olympos' dazzling splendour.   610
> Soon and forever,
> as in all past time, this law
> will hold; no human being gains
> great wealth without disaster.

(**B2**)   Hope wanders far and wide,   615
  brings benefit to many – but
  to others the false lure of empty needs;
  it creeps up on someone who does not know
  until he's burnt his foot on the hot fire.
  A wise man said these famous words: 620
  evil seems good when the god leads
  someone to destruction; but the humble
  man survives without disaster.   625

Perhaps the first point to be made, for those approaching such an ode in the rehearsal room, is that it is performed in character, by a choros of Councillors who are enmeshed in the action of the play; it is *their* reflection on what they have just seen, not Sophocles' own authorial commentary. And indeed it will emerge that the Councillors' reflection is inadequate as a response to the preceding scene. They are out of their depth from the moment when the Guard brings back Antigone, caught burying Polyneikes, until after the prophet Teiresias has departed, having given Kreon a terrible warning that leads him to turn to them for advice (1091ff.).

In the original Greek, the ode was structured into two pairs of metrically matching stanzas, here marked A1/A2 and B1/B2. There is, as often in choral odes, a strong difference between the two pairs, which should be emphasized by a change in the music and the choreography; in the A stanzas the Councillors focus on the sufferings of the royal house of Thebes, while in the B stanzas they contemplate the power of Zeus and the dangers that surround mortals.

After the tremendous tension of the preceding scene, this ode begins as a subdued meditation on the disasters that can affect families. But the sea-imagery of the A1 stanza soon invites an energetic response from the choreographer. In A2 the Councillors home in upon their own royal house of Thebes, and the stanza divides in two after 598; both halves lead to grim conclusions, the second perhaps alluding, in its mention of 'crazy speech', to the rash words that they have heard hurled between Kreon and the sisters in the previous scene. In the later Scene 5, which begins as a lyric interchange between Antigone and the Councillors, they will accuse her of 'going to the limits of daring' (853), and of destroying herself by being 'obstinate and wilful' (874–5); but there has been nothing irrational in her words, no trace of Furies in Antigone's mind during the scene that has now just been enacted – merely passionate devotion to what she believes to be right. So, the Councillors may already be misunderstanding the heroine.

In B1 the mood changes; the Councillors proclaim the power of Zeus, and then affirm an old belief that: 'no human being gains/great wealth without disaster' (613–14). The Elders of Aeschylus' *Agamemnon* knew better; they explicitly rejected this belief (*Agamemnon* 750ff.). They sang that they, apart from others, are sure that it is *impiety* that breeds destruction, not wealth in itself. The contrasting naivety of Sophocles' Councillors needs to be brought out in the choreography; it is precisely because Kreon has acted impiously in refusing burial to Polyneikes and condemning Antigone to death that he causes the suicides of his son and his wife. All that will be spelled out by the prophet Teiresias in Scene 6 (cf. esp. 1064ff.).

The B2 stanza is ominous. Again as in A1, a powerful image is used to reinforce the point of the first five lines: '[Hope's false lure] creeps up on someone who does not know/until he's burnt his foot on the hot fire' (618–19). Both this pair of lines and the closing four lines of the ode (620ff.) are prophetic of Kreon's fate – but the Councillors do not realize this until the Finale, when Kreon brings back the body of his son and is then confronted by the corpse of his wife Eurydike, who killed herself when she learnt of Haimon's suicide. Kreon himself is present in the playing space throughout this ode, so the idea that some of the Councillors' thoughts may apply to him is encouraged.[53]

---

[53]In my production, Kreon sat during this choros at a small table just outside the circular playing space EBR, smoking a cigarette and drinking a shot glass of raki.

This ode requires the choreographer to respond to the overall trend of thought in each stanza, which I have analysed above; she or he may also choose to have the dance respond mimetically to specific passages of imagery, for example the sea surge in A1, in A2 the god striking the generations down and later the bloody knife of the gods of the underworld, and the creeping up of the false lure of Hope in B2. These same parameters – attention both to the thoughts expressed in the lyrics, and to details of the imagery in which those thoughts are clothed – are essential when approaching any choral ode in Greek tragedy and developing movement for it.

3.5.2.2 A lyric scene

Near the beginning of Sophocles' *Elektra*, Elektra comes out of the palace, dressed in shabby clothes, and in a wide-ranging lyric monody (86ff.) she laments the murder of her father and the failure of her brother Orestes to return and avenge it, and expresses her isolation and her determination to persevere. She is then joined by the Women of Argos, and the first Choros is not delivered, as usual, entirely by the choros; in this play it is a *kommos* – a lyric lamentation shared by a soloist with the choros.[54] Here is the first part of that *kommos*:

Women (A1)   Elektra, daughter of   121
      the worst of mothers,
      why do you always shriek aloud
      insatiable grief for Agamemnon
      godlessly destroyed so long ago   125
      by your deceitful mother's tricks?
      Her wicked hand betrayed him. If it's right to say,
      I wish the man who planned all this was dead.

---

[54]For a similar lyric scene on the entry of the choros cf. Euripides' *Medea* 131ff. In the great *kommos* in Aeschylus' *Libation Bearers* (306–478), the choros is joined by two soloists, the reunited Orestes and Elektra.

Elektra Daughters of noble parents,
you have come to console me.   130
I understand what you are saying, it does not
escape me; but I do not want to let this go,
stop mourning for my pitiable father.
You are my dearest friends, we have shared
every kind of joy; but please, allow me to   135
be crazed by grief.

Women (A2)   All right – but groans and prayers will
    never
resurrect your father from the stagnant
pond of Haides where we all must go.
At first your feelings were appropriate – but now   140
by constant lamentation you destroy yourself
in hopeless pain which cannot cure your sufferings.
Why d'you reach out for the intolerable?
Elektra   Only a fool forgets   145
parents who have died wretchedly.
The grieving nightingale lives in my mind,
the bird of utter desolation, Zeus' messenger,
Always crying out for Itys, Itys.
All-suffering Niobe, I worship you;   150
frozen to stone,
you weep for evermore.

Women (B1)   Look, girl, you aren't
the only one this grief
has come upon; why is it worse   155
for you than for your other siblings?
Chrysothemis still lives, and Iphianassa,
and the noble man good Fortune
sheltered in childhood from this pain;   160
this famous land of Mykenai will one day
welcome him when he comes home,
his steps endorsed by Zeus – Orestes!
Elektra   Yes – the man I wait for, never-resting, childless,
miserable, husbandless; I waste away,   165

drenched in my tears, fated
for never-ending grief! – while he forgets
both what he's suffered and what he's been told.
I get his messages – but they are lies!   170
He says he longs to come – but never thinks
it's worth his while to actually appear.

Women (B2)   Take courage, girl, take courage.
Zeus is still great in heaven; he looks down
on everything, and has great power.   175
Yield your excessive anger up to him; do not
forget your enemies, nor hate them overmuch.
Time is a kindly god.
The son of Agamemnon lives in   180
Krisa, grazing-place beside the sea.
He won't forget; nor will his father, now
a god, a king in Haides' halls.
Elektra   What about me? Most of my life has gone,   185
and left me without hope; I can't hold out.
I waste away; I have no children,
no man is my friend and fights for me.
I'm like a worthless foreign slave,
housemaid in my father's rooms, wearing   190
these shabby clothes, waiting in hope
there'll be some leftovers for me to eat.

The *kommos* positively invites division between individual
members of the choros.[55] In this Choros the Women are not a
monolithic unity; they provide a set of individual voices, and
different perspectives on the action. Right from the start they
challenge Elektra's determined fixity in grief; and the *kommos*
demands a complex choreographic response to the ebb and
flow of the lyric debate, since the soloists in their seven stanzas
display seven different responses to Elektra; in order, severe
and authoritative (A1), bright and firm (A2), tough and

---

[55]The following analysis is adapted from Ewans (ed.) 2000: 186–8.

energetic (B1), almost naively optimistic (B2) and, in the remainder of the Choros, knowledgeable and sympathetic (C1), passionately challenging (C2) and concerned (C3). These seven danced interventions create a balance; by the end, Elektra retains the Women's sympathy, while they have still made it clear that her position is extreme – and, to some of them, untenable.

The keynote is struck at once. The Women are Elektra's friends; and the choreography needs to establish this immediately, by close physical contact. The first Woman makes it clear that she is on Elektra's side; but she does not understand why their friend continues her lamentations far beyond their due period. It is not rational or reasonable (this can be conveyed by the other choros members supporting her in this dance); and Elektra must concede the point at once (135–6), interacting with the Women. They should take up her mood, and echo it in their movements during her response. When the performer of the Women's A2 stanza develops this attack (cf. esp. 140ff.), Elektra must retreat before dancing a powerful defence, choosing two heroines from myth – Prokne and Niobe – both of whom are fixed for evermore in their grief; but she does not convince the Women at all. In the B1 stanza, the next Woman continues to object, naming Elektra's siblings. Elektra ignores the mention of her sisters, but the optimistic description of Orestes leads her to exhibit her anger and her loss of hope.

The B2 stanza is even more optimistic than B1; the Woman who performs it has faith in Zeus, and in Time – the one *daimōn* in whom Elektra has none, since a seemingly endless period of defiance and suffering has not brought Orestes back. The singer/speaker should move forward to a commanding position, and attempt to involve Elektra in a dance of happiness; but Elektra rejects this, and becomes isolated; 185ff. are the fullest declaration of her hopelessness. As the lyric scene proceeds further, beyond the extract which I have examined here, there are a few moments when Elektra might seem to join with the Women (C1, 194ff.); but when one Woman expresses sympathy (C3), Elektra's closing stanza leaves her in a mood of defiance and determination, isolated from the Women by her misery. Only in the dialogue scene which follows, led off by a further expression of sympathy from the Women and a long speech from Elektra, do they come closer together.

3.5.2.3 A lyric/dialogue scene

In Aeschylus' tragedy, Agamemnon has walked into the palace over the robes (**3.4.1.4**). Kassandra remains silent in the chariot while the Elders express their disquiet in Choros 4. She is then still, silent and motionless when Klytaimestra comes out and orders her to go inside the palace (Scene 5: 1036ff.). Frustrated and furious, Klytaimestra will not waste any more time being ignored, and returns indoors.

After this, Kassandra, who has been present but silent for 290 lines, in breach of the conventions of the Greek stage, suddenly leaps from the chariot and bursts into extremely agitated song; it will therefore attract the closest attention from the audience. Here is the text of the first, lyric/dialogue portion of the scene, in which at first individual Elders respond in spoken words to Kassandra's lyric outbursts. As the interaction is complex, I have placed all the originally sung words in italics:

> **Kassandra (A1)**   *(shrieks) Ah!*
> *Oh Apollo, Apollo!*
> **1 Elder**   Why do you cry and name Apollo?
> He's not a god whom anyone lamenting should
> approach.   1075
> **Kassandra (A2)**   *(shrieks) Ah!*
> *Oh Apollo, Apollo!*
> **1 Elder**   Now once again she cries out ominously to
> the god who cannot listen to a plaintive song.
> **Kassandra (B1)**   *Oh Apollo, Apollo,*
> *god of the ways, and my destroyer,*   1080
> *once again you have destroyed me easily.*

1 Elder   I think she's going to prophesy about her
      miseries;
   the god's gift stays with her, although she's a slave.
Kassandra (B2)   *Oh Apollo, Apollo,*
         god of the ways, and my destroyer.   1085
         Ah! Where have you led me? To what house?
1 Elder   The house of the Atreidai; if you don't know
      that
   I can inform you; then you will not speak it false.
Kassandra (C1)   *A house that hates the gods, and*
            knows   1090
            inside its heart murder of kindred, severed
               heads –
            a slaughterhouse, a floor sprinkled with blood.
1 Elder   The foreign girl is like a hunting dog, keen
      on the scent.
   She searches for the track of murder; she will find it,
      too.
Kassandra (C2)   *Yes, I believe this evidence –*   1095
         the baby children who lament
         their slaughter, and their roasted flesh their
            father ate.
1 Elder   We certainly have heard of your prophetic gifts;
   but we want no predictions here today.
Kassandra (D1)   *Oh god, what's being plotted?*
            What   1100
         is this new grief? Great evil's
         planned here in this house,
         unbearable to all its friends, impossible to cure;
         and help stands far away.
1 Elder   I cannot understand this prophecy; as for the
      others,   1105
   I knew them; all of Argos cries them out.
Kassandra (D2)   *Oh wretched woman, is this your*
            design?
         To wash your husband in a ritual bath,
         then – how shall I speak the end?

It will come quickly – look, she reaches out,   1110
stretches each hand in turn.
1 Elder   I don't yet understand; for now after her riddles
I am bewildered by these obscure oracles.
Kassandra (E1)   *Oh God, Oh God, what's this?*
A net of death?   1115
But no, the snare's the partner in his bed
and in his murder; in this family insatiable strife
must cry a victory-song for sacrifice to be
avenged.
1 Elder   What kind of Fury do you ask to raise her cry
over this house? Your words bring me no joy.   1120
Elders   *But to the heart the saffron drop*
runs fast, the blood which for men speared
reaches its end as life's sun sets.
Destruction quickly comes.
Kassandra (E2)   *Ah! Ah! Keep the bull*   1125
from the cow. She's tangled him
in robes, a black-horned thing.
She strikes; he falls into the water.
I tell you the treachery that happens in the bath.
1 Elder   I would not boast that I am really good   1130
at understanding prophecies; but this I do not like.
Elders   *What happy word for mankind*
ever comes from oracles? Only through
misfortune
do the wordy crafts of prophets bring
their tales of terror for us all to learn.   1135
Kassandra (F1)   *Oh! What about my miserable, evil fate?*
I cry aloud, pouring out my own sufferings as
well.
Why did you bring me here in all my misery,
except to die with him? What else?
Elders   *You're frenzied, carried from us by the gods,*   1140
as you cry your own tuneless elegy,
just like the tawny nightingale whose miserable
heart

laments unendingly for her dead son
slaughtered by both his parents.
Kassandra (F2)   *I wish my fate were like*   1145
the tuneful nightingale's; the gods gave her
a feathered shape and sweet life free from pain;
I will be cloven by a double-sided blade.
Elders   *Which god impels these rushing stabs*   1150
of useless inspiration? Why do you
mould to a melody of dissonant and piercing
strain
such fearful things?
Who marked for you the limits of this path
of ill-omened prophecy?   1155
Kassandra (G1)   *Oh Paris, when you married you*
destroyed your family!
Skamander, river of my native land,
beside your banks I once was nursed and grew
unhappy;
now it seems I soon will prophesy   1160
around the rivers Acheron and Kokytos.
Elders   *This is all too clear! Why do you say*
such things a baby child could understand?
A deadly sting attacks me as you cry
so pitiably for your dreadful fate,   1165
It breaks my heart to hear.
Kassandra (G2)   *Oh pain, pain of my city utterly*
destroyed,
and sacrifice my father made before the walls
so rich in slaughter of the grazing flocks.
There was no cure to save   1170
my city from its fate;
and I will swiftly fall warm-blooded to the ground.
Elders   *This follows what you said before;*
and some malignant daimōn weighs so heavily
he forces you to sing of miserable suffering and
death;   1175
I cannot see how this will end.

As Kassandra explains to the Elders later, in the spoken part of the scene (1202ff.), she accepted the gift of prophecy from Apollo, but then betrayed him.[56] Apollo could not take back his gift, so instead he punished her that her prophecies, though true, would never be believed. This legend would be known to the majority of the audience; it is, however, not initially known to the Elders of Argos, so in this lyric dialogue they are all too familiar with the past events in their city, far distant from Kassandra's homeland, which she describes with a prophetess' insight – the banquet of his children's flesh served by Atreus to Thyestes – but quite unable to understand her as she sees Klytaimestra's preparations to murder Agamemnon in his ritual bath.[57]

Aeschylus dramatizes Kassandra's response to this situation, in which she herself knows that she will be killed, through a formidable control of form. Her lyric outcries begin simply with pain-laden shrieks followed by calls upon the god who is destroying her (the identical A1 and A2); then B1 and B2 are more coherent, still identical for their first two lines but diverging in the third. In the C stanzas she responds for the first time to the comments of an individual Elder; he tells her prosaically that she is in front of the house of the Atreidai, and in these two stanzas she describes it as the slaughterhouse that it is. This puts the Elders, who are already seriously disturbed (Choros 4), on the defensive:

> We certainly have heard of your prophetic gifts;
> but we want no predictions here today.

(1098–9)

---

[56]See Kovacs 1987.

[57]Aeschylus has been deliberately saving any mention of the hideous past of the house of Atreus for this moment, concentrating instead, earlier in the play, on the sacrifice of Iphigenia and the loss of many men at Troy. Now Kassandra prepares the audience for Aigisthos, the surviving son of Thyestes, to enter the picture, taking revenge on Atreus' son Agamemnon for Atreus' murder of his siblings.

However, Kassandra is not to be stopped. She segues from the past to the immediate future, and in the D stanzas sees a vision of new slaughter, the 'wretched woman' (1107) who is planning death in a bath. As she sings this, the curse of Apollo works at once; two different Elders say that they cannot understand this prophecy (1105–6 and 1112–13). In the E1 stanza, Kassandra sees a net of death, and Agamemnon's wife as his murderess; and though they do not understand, the Elders are moved by the height of her emotion. One Elder speaks an ominous couplet (1119–20); and then the whole choros suddenly takes voice, as they express their fear of the destruction that Kassandra has prophesied ('But to the heart the saffron drop/ runs fast'; 1121–2). In the original Greek they now sing, as Kassandra has been and is singing, the dochmiac – the metre of the utmost excitement. This shows how deeply she has disturbed them.

Kassandra continues relentlessly in E2, directly addressing the Elders for the first time ('I tell you the treachery that happens in the bath', 1129); gradually she is becoming released from the lash of the visions and develops into a more reflective mood. This stanza evokes just one more spoken comment from an individual Elder (1130–1, a masterpiece of understatement); then the whole group sings again, and no Elder speaks after this; the exchange remains, in the original, entirely sung by both Kassandra and the Elders until it ends.

In F1, Kassandra, for the first time, laments her own miserable fate; and the Elders then, also for the first time, try to engage fully with her (1140ff.). They succeed; in F2 Kassandra responds to what they have sung, lamenting that unlike the nightingale she herself will be savagely murdered. However, the communication breaks down; the Elders ask her why she is uttering such ill-omened prophecies (1150ff.); but she ignores them in the G stanzas, lamenting how Paris has destroyed his family, will kill her too and left her city of Troy to a terrible fate. Even though the Elders are heartbroken by what they hear (1164–6), she is now wrapped up in herself and her impending death.

But this is not the end of the scene, which Richard Wagner once declared to be 'the most perfect thing mortal art has ever produced'.[58] Kassandra recovers enough to move to spoken words, and tries, twice attacked by the agony of prophetic insight (1214 and 1256), to convey directly to the Elders who cannot believe her that Klytaimestra will kill both Agamemnon and herself. Furthermore, she prophesies the return of Orestes to avenge them. Then she goes in to her death with great dignity and courage.

In the first lyric/dialogue section of this scene, we see Aeschylus using form – the gradual expansion and increasing coherence of Kassandra's utterances, and the development of the Elders from individual spoken comments to an intense mass lyric response to Kassandra's visions – to shape the audience's understanding of how she develops from an incoherent expression of agony through increasingly clear prophecies to a lament for herself and all the Trojans. She takes the Elders with her, even though they are debarred from understanding her prophecies of the future; they move from their initial objectivity and their wish not to hear her through to compassion for her fate. No production of this scene can succeed unless it is attuned to the journeys that Kassandra and the Elders undergo, and the way in which they are underpinned by Aeschylus' use of the formal structures of Greek lyric verse.[59]

---

[58]C. Wagner 1978: 805. Entry for 18 November 1874.

[59]My own production in 1986 was flawed. A powerful, continuous electronic soundscape accompanied the whole of the lyric/dialogue section of the scene, including the Elders' spoken words; and not enough was made of the moment when the whole choros of Elders are galvanized into song. It was only saved by the electrifying performance of the then student Jan Hunt in the role of Kassandra; she subsequently went on to a fulfilling career as a professional actress. YouTube 'Aeschylus' *Agamemnon* (1986 production)', starting at 58.59.

3.5.2.4 Conclusion

Whether sung or (as I prefer) spoken in a modern production, the words of a Greek choral lyric are paramount. Choroses are not interludes, but a complementary form of expression that advances the action between dialogue scenes. Accordingly, they should never be cut. Choreography and musical accompaniment must be carefully handled; they are essential, but must support, not overwhelm, the words. A delicate balance is needed to bring off a successful production of a Choros in a Greek tragedy.[60]

3.5.3 The comic choros

3.5.3.1 A choros divided

This example of a comic Choros comes at the midpoint of Aristophanes' *Lysistrata*, just after Lysistrata has vanquished the Bureaucrat in the *agōn* and sent him away to die. It takes the place of the normal central *parabasis* (an address to the citizens; see below **3.5.3.2**) because the divided choros groups of Old Men and Old Women are not yet reconciled; but it does have one feature in common with a *parabasis*; the lyric stanzas are interspersed with dialogue. To make this clear I have once again printed the originally sung and danced portions in italics.

CHOROS 3

1 Old Man   Now is the time for all free men to rise.
    Take off your cloaks, gentlemen; get ready for action.   615

---

[60]Danny Scheie's richly inventive Santa Cruz production of Mary-Kay Gamel's Euripides translation *Orestes Terrorist* in 2011 was outstanding in many respects; but the loud band music that accompanied the sung and danced parts made most of the words of the choroses and lyric solos inaudible. This severely limited the overall effectiveness of the performance. My own composer and choreographer in Sophocles' *Elektra* (1998) did not go that far; but in retrospect both the music and the dancing were sometimes too vigorous or intrusive, at the expense of full absorption of the words by the audience.

Old Men (A1)   *This business has the stench*
                of something sinister; I smell a whiff
                of tyranny. And I'm afraid some Spartans   620
                may have met here in secret to incite
                these women, hated by the gods,
                to seize the treasure; that's the jury pay
                on which I live.   625
1 Old Man   It's terrible that they are telling us, the
        citizens,
    what we must do – women just babbling on about the
        war –
    and making peace with Spartans,
    whom I trust less than hungry wolves.
    They're weaving a net of tyranny.   630
    I will not endure it; I will stand on guard
    and sing heroic songs of victory.
    I will parade in arms like the great tyrant-killer
    and strike the same pose as his statue – nicely placed
    to hit this horrible old woman on the jaw.   635

1 Old Woman   Your own mother won't recognize you
        if you do.
    Take off your cloaks, dear ladies.
Old Women (A2)   *Citizens, we will begin*
                with words of value to the city.
                This is just, because the city nourished us   640
                in luxury and comfort.
                When I was seven, I served the goddess for eight
                    months,
                I ground corn for the sacred cakes at ten, and then
                    stripped off
                my saffron robe, and went through rites of
                    passage before puberty.   645
                And when I was a beautiful young woman,
                    I carried
                the sacred basket, wearing a necklace made
                    of figs.

1 Old Woman   So don't I have a duty to give the city
good advice?
Do not begrudge me, just because I am a woman,
if I bring changes for the better.   650
I have contributed my share; I've borne you sons.
You miserable old men have not contributed;
you squandered all the wealth your ancestors had won
from war with Persia, and you've not made up the
deficit.
Indeed, we're going bankrupt thanks to you.   655
D'you dare to grumble? Don't annoy us,
or I will use my boot to kick you on the jaw.

Old Men (B1)   *This is a total outrage!*
– and it's getting worse.   660
Now is the time for every man with balls to fight.
Off with your shirts; a man should smell
just like a man, and not be wrapped away.
Come on, foot soldiers,   665
just as we went to battle when
we were still young.
We must rise up again, take wing   670
and slough off this old skin.

1 Old Man   If we give them even a tiny chance,
there's nothing slippery that they won't do;
they will build ships, and try to fight
at sea against us, like the Karian queen.   675
And if they turn to horses, we won't have a chance;
women just love horses and mounting up,
and they don't fall off. Think of the Amazons,
whom Mikon painted fighting men on horseback.
We've got to get them all and put them   680
in the stocks – so grab their necks!

Old Women (B2)   *If you inflame me, I'll let loose*
my inner sow on you, and shear your fleece.
You'll beg your friends to save your shorn-off
carcasses.   685

> *We'll strip for action too,*
> *so we will smell like women mad enough to bite.*
> *Come on, attack me, if you never want*   690
> *to eat garlic again*
> *or chew black beans.*
> *Just one bad word – I'm so enraged –*
> *and I will crush your nuts.*   695

1 Old Woman   I don't give a shit for you, as long as
        Lampito still lives
and that dear noble girl from Thebes, Ismenia.
No matter if you voted seven times, you are quite
        powerless –
you wretched man whom all your neighbours hate.
Only yesterday I tried to have a party   700
for the local wives and kids. I sent an invite to
a dear and special friend from Boiotia – an eel;
but they said they could not send her, because of your
        decrees.
You won't stop voting stupidly, until one of us grabs
        your leg,
gives a good heave, and breaks your neck.   705

Aristophanes' choros in this play is evenly divided – in the original production, twelve Old Men squaring off against twelve Old Women; and after their entrance they settle down, each half-choros sitting during the dialogue scenes on one side of the playing space. If you have an arena stage, they should sit around the front perimeter with their backs to the audience, so as not to pull focus from the scene that they, like the audience, are watching. A proscenium arch stage presents challenges with where to 'park' the choros between Choroses; cf. **3.6**.

After Lysistrata and her women have gone back into the citadel represented by the *skēnē* just before this Choros, the Old Men and Old Women rise up and each group occupies one half of the playing space. The Old Men are in the left segment, since they entered first from the left *eisodos* and transited around the perimeter of the *orchēstra*, as they mimed climbing up to the Acropolis, to arrive from the right in front of the *skēnē* doors; they were then driven into the left segment by the Old Women, who pursued them and threw buckets of water at them. The Old Women would therefore naturally occupy the right segment after *their* entrance and their successful attack on the Old Men.[61]

This Choros is formally structured; four danced lyric stanzas (A1, A2; B1, B2) are each followed by spoken dialogue from individual choros members. In both the A and B sets of stanzas, the Old Men lead off with a stanza and a speech, then the Old Women respond with a stanza and a speech of their own. In addition to this, each stanza in the A group is introduced by a pair of spoken lines; the emotional temperature is relatively low at the beginning of the Choros.

This Choros is at the mid-point of the play, where a *parabasis*, an address to the audience (**3.5.3.2**), would normally take place; but the Old Men are in no position to advise the citizens of Athens about anything; they therefore express suspicion that the women are aiming at tyranny (which nothing in the play so far would justify); and when they claim to be as tough as the tyrannicides of the sixth century, a single threat from one of the women (636–7) is enough to make them be quiet. But as yet neither side has invaded the other's half of the playing space.

This situation continues into the A2 stanza, where the Old Women do seem for a moment to be performing a mini-*parabasis* of their own, as the stanza is very like one key element of the *parabasis*, an address in character to the audience. It is clear – and should be made clear in the movement – that the Old Women are winning the argument in this stanza and subsequent speech; they emphasize in the lyrics the rituals by which they became adult female citizens, and in the solo speech the Old Woman picks up Lysistrata's passionate charge in the preceding scene that the men are sending their sons off

---

[61]Parts of the following analysis are drawn from Ewans 2010: 238–40.

to die (588ff.). She concludes with another physical threat, which should of course be mimed; this speech invites at least this one Old Woman (maybe more) to invade the men's half of the playing space, albeit temporarily.

The Old Men and the Old Women both took off their cloaks in preparation for this ode (617, 637); now the Old Men take off their shirts as well, and call each other to battle stations. (The B1 stanza admits that the men cannot reply in rational words to the women's argument, though in the speech that follows they could advance physically on the women.) In response (B2), the Old Women threaten to strip for action too – though being more modest they do not actually do so;[62] and they dare the men to attack them – an offer which is not taken up! Both 694–5 and 704–5 provide an opportunity for a vigorous mime in the choreography, which leaves the Old Women in the ascendant and the Old Men scared and defeated. The Old Women could therefore use the B2 stanza and the speech that follows it to invade the Old Men's half of the playing space and drive them back to their 'parked' position. The women are then in the middle of their triumphant return to *their* normal position ready for the next scene when Lysistrata enters, interacting directly with one of them as she enacts (comically) in her words and gestures the high despair of a tragic heroine.

3.5.3.2 *The* parabasis

A *parabasis* is literally a 'coming-forward'; the choros advances out of the play, but not normally out of character, and addresses the audience on matters of immediate topical resonance. Typically there is one in each comedy, located towards the mid-point; but in some plays Aristophanes presents two *parabaseis*. There is no *parabasis* in either of his last two, fourth-century plays, *Assemblywomen* and *Wealth*, in both of which the role of the choros is much diminished in comparison

---

[62]They are clearly fully dressed except for their cloaks in Scene 6, while the Old Men are not.

with the plays that Aristophanes created before the Athenians lost the Peloponnesian War.

The problem of the *parabasis* is that its focus on current affairs may make it inaccessible to a modern audience; but there are strategies that can overcome this. One of the best examples of a *parabasis* is the famous one in *Frogs* (674ff.), which led to the unique honour for this play that it was revived the year after its first performance because of the advice in the *parabasis*. I shall describe it, and then set out a possible way to perform it today.

The Initiates' *parabasis* in *Frogs* is in four parts: two short lyrics each followed by one long speech. The first lyric mocks a politician who was doubtless in the audience, Kleophon, for his cowardice and his funny accent. Then comes a speech appealing for those men who took the wrong side in the events of 411 BCE, when an oligarchic government of 'The Four Hundred' overthrew the democracy, only to be evicted in its turn, to be restored to full citizenship:

> But if we swell with pride and think we are too grand for
>   this –
> especially now the city's tossed by storms – then in
> the future men will see that we were wrong.
>
> (703–5)

Next there is a stanza with further abuse – this time of the 'monkey', 'little Kleigenes' – and the Initiates prophesy that he will come to a speedy end. Finally, one of them embarks on a second speech, this one drawing an analogy between the better citizens and the 'ancient silver coinage' – men whom the city doesn't use, although they are: 'well born/and wise, and just, and good, and fair, /trained in the wrestling-school, music and dance'; instead it uses 'base bronze / – slaves, migrants, criminals and men from families of criminals' (727–31). The *parabasis* ends with a plea to Athens to change its ways and use its best men once again.

Despite being composed for a specific occasion in a particular city in 405 BCE, the two speeches have deep resonance for any modern democracy; the first one advising reconciliation between political enemies, and the second one the appointment of upstanding, not corrupt men to political office. (When I drafted this part of the book in the dying days of the Trump presidency [2020], both speeches seemed particularly relevant to the USA.) My advice to a director of *Frogs* would be either to simply omit the abusive lyrics about Kleophon and Kleigenes, or replace each of them with a short, snappy denunciation of a contemporary politician, local or national, who is well known to your own audience. But beware of the modern laws of slander![63]

3.5.3.3 Conclusion

As you will have seen with my example of Choros 3 from *Lysistrata,* a comic choral lyric makes varied and considerable demands on the composer and choreographer; and as with tragedy, they must strike a fine balance, taking care not to pull focus from the all-important words. Words in Greek comedy, as in tragedy, even in lyric sections, express the unfolding emotions of the characters and are, as a result, the essential clues on the basis of which the music and the action must be developed.

3.6 Performing Greek drama on an end-on stage

3.6.1 Comedy: *Peace* (2009)

The first time I directed a Greek play on a proscenium arch stage was with Aristophanes' *Peace.*[64] The studio in which I

---

[63]For a response to a more complex *parabasis*, the first one in *Peace*, cf. Ewans 2011: 253–4.

[64]Co-directed by Elizabeth Smyth.

had created a half-size replica of the Greek theatre shape for previous productions was impossible to use because there was no space backstage for the giant flying dung-beetle that is essential for this play; and indeed the beetle created problems even in the proscenium arch theatre that we used for the production, since there was no fly tower and accordingly no resources for flying it in and out. We solved this problem by having the beetle appear on a hydraulic lift on a raised platform, with the stage machinist to whom Trygaios cries out when the beetle starts to lurch in mid-air visibly operating the controls from behind it (173ff.).[65]

Our theatre had a proscenium arch with an approximately two-metre thrust in front of it; two sets of steps, one on each side, descended from the thrust into the space in the auditorium in front of the audience. (This space was approximately two metres deep, from the edge of the stage to the front row of seats.) Our first move was to bring the action forward by painting on the stage a patterned golden circular area as the main playing space, almost half of which was in front of the proscenium arch, on the forestage. We then placed the *skēnē* façade immediately behind that circle, leaving room backstage for the stones with which the gods have allowed War to bury Peace, and for Peace herself to emerge, after the Farmers have demolished this barrier, on a throne on a small *ekkuklēma*.

Marking out the golden circle also enabled us to use the space outside and in front of it. A spotlight was installed to illuminate the area stage right front of the circle, allowing for lines to be delivered to the audience – as for example when the

---

[65]Stagehands also need to be visible later in this play, when the Farmers, about to perform the first *parabasis*, ask them to take their tools and guard them carefully against thieves who hang around the theatre (729ff.). We assigned two stagehands to hold the box of vegetables, and the mortar, which War uses in 236ff. Of course, the stagehands all wore black to indicate that they were not part of the cast. In the original Athenian productions, I would conjecture that stagehands were marked out by wearing everyday clothes *and being unmasked*.

Second Slave addressed them at 43ff.; the First Slave then left the circle and came forward to extreme front centre (also lit by a spotlight) to tell the audience the backstory at 50ff. And the front right spotlight was used by Trygaios for his asides during War's terrifying appearance at 236ff., and elsewhere.

All the action had of necessity to be brought forward, and of course actors had to face towards the audience as much as possible. So, for example, the scene between Trygaios and Hermes, when he arrives at Zeus' house, could be played as normal on a proscenium arch stage – with both actors fairly far forward, and 'cheating' lines out to the audience. But it turned out that certain scenes in which this was impossible played perfectly, since ours was a small theatre with good acoustics – for example, the scene where the Farmers, spurred on by Hermes, haul Peace out of the cave upstage; it was simply necessary to make sure that no section went on very long without at least one of the actors turning towards the audience.

The positioning of the choros was the principal problem. The normal 'parked' position in the ancient theatre – seated in front of the front rows of the audience – was impossible in this theatre; so, we placed them on the stage left perimeter of the circular playing space. From there they could be seen to be engaged with the action; however it was necessary for them to remain seated and still when not taking part in a scene, so as not to pull focus. Fortunately, the choros of Farmers in this play has a great deal to do, with the scene where they haul out Peace, choral odes both long and short, two *parabaseis* and frequent interactions with Trygaios during the spoken scenes.

One innovation that greatly enhanced the production was the use of the house lights. They went up whenever characters addressed the audience – as they quite often do; for just one example take Trygaios' lines on returning from Olympos:

You looked quite small from right up there;
from heaven you looked a pretty rotten lot,
and here you look much worse!

(821ff.)

And, of course, the house lights went up again when Trygaios presents Festival to one of the Councillors in the audience (906ff.),[66] and during both *parabaseis* – though these included complex dancing and some lighting special effects on the stage as well as an address to the audience. Also at 539ff., where Hermes brings Trygaios to the very front of the stage and invites him to look into the audience, and guess by their attitude to the attainment of Peace what trades they ply. By doing this we subverted the 'fourth wall' and involved the audience in the play, reviving as best we could the communal aspect of the ancient audience in their *theatron*; our audiences did not merely watch the play as isolated individuals in the darkness, but had to become aware of each other as part of a community of spectators.

A great deal of the action was performed at or near the centre of the circle; for example, the altar on which Trygaios makes offerings was placed there, with the barbecue immediately behind it, for 937ff. But we did not hesitate to use the front of the playing space, as in a proscenium arch theatre it is not the weak position that it is in the Greek theatre shape but a position of power. So, for example, when later in that scene Hierokles the oracle-seller attempted to grab some of the feast for himself, Trygaios conducted the dialogue with him in the front half, while the Second Slave tended to the feast on the barbecue just behind the centre-point of the circle. When Hierokles became insufferable, the Second Slave and Trygaios drove him off with blows of a stick, chasing him around the front of the playing space and off stage right. We naturally used the conventions of the ancient theatre for entries and exits, with stage right leading to the country and stage left to the downtown of wherever the location is. That location changes three times, from in front of Trygaios' house to in front of Zeus', to the mouth of the cave where War has

---

[66]On one night of the run, the Chancellor of the university was in attendance; it was irresistible for the actor playing Trygaios (who knew him personally) to present this august figure with the near-naked girl and seat her on his lap. He thoroughly enjoyed the production.

imprisoned Peace, and then back again to in front of Trygaios' house. But we left the façade the same throughout, and this did not seem to disturb the audience.

These are the main features of the way in which we adapted one of the most difficult surviving Greek plays for a successful run in an end-on theatre.[67]

3.6.2 Tragedy: *Medea* (2021)

This tragedy was performed on a smallish proscenium arch stage with no thrust, in a theatre with an audience capacity of 144. The set consisted of the façade of a house upstage, with one set of double doors at the centre. There was also a window, which had a blind behind it but no glass, so that the offstage dialogue that is so important in this play – Medea's outcries in Scene 1 and Choros 1, and the boys' cries for help and death-shrieks during Choros 6 – could be heard clearly. And there was a raised platform upstage right, for Medea's final appearance.

In front of the façade there was a playing space seven metres wide and five metres deep. Two benches were placed far downstage at the extreme right and left, on a diagonal facing into the playing area. These were for the Women of Corinth to sit on when not taking part in the action. There were four Women, two each side; and as all the odes in this play are four stanzas long, it was possible to distribute the parts evenly. In this production, music (an electronic soundscape) was only heard when Euripides' original text was in lyric metres; and all choros lines were spoken by individuals, except the last line of the play ('That's how this story ends.'), which was declaimed in unison.

This tight performance space, together with the modern dress costumes, transformed *Medea* from a spectacle for a vast open-air theatre into a contemporary chamber play, confined between the two black side walls of the stage and the façade of

---

[67]To view the production, enter Aristophanes' 'Peace' (2009 production) on YouTube. For more details of the play's staging problems and how we overcame them cf. Ewans 2011: 240–64.

Medea's house. Our aim was to foster an intensity at least as powerful as that of one of Strindberg's domestic dramas, by a constant flow between Scenes and Choroses and a steady build-up to and beyond the climactic murder of the children. Intimate contact could be made – for example when one of the Women tries to console Medea:

> Your sufferings have made you miserable,
> unhappy woman;
> where will you turn? What friend,
> what house, what land will save you from your troubles?
> The gods have thrown you, Medea,
> into a surge of troubles that can't be escaped.

> (358–63)

It was possible and desirable for the Woman speaking this stanza to approach and touch Medea. (A similar tactic was used at 996ff., and with the same individual speaking both of these stanzas she was marked out as even more sympathetic to Medea than the other Women.) Indeed, developing particular attitudes for different members of the choros, by assigning lines to each cast member according to their individual 'character' or attitude, can be very helpful in modern productions of both tragedy and comedy; it helps the choros members to orient their contribution to the play.

As in *Peace*, some passages that directly address the audience were played with the house lights raised. The aim was once again to break down the 'fourth wall' and make the audience feel that they were something of a community sharing in the drama (like the ancient Athenians in broad daylight), rather than watching the play as isolated individuals kept apart from each other by being in darkness. This device was used in the Nurse's opening exposition (6–45), during the 'sufferings of women' section of Medea's first address to the Women of Corinth (230–51, the passage used by the suffragettes) and for the Messenger (from 1167 to the end of his speech). Audience address was also used by the Women in their Choral Interlude at 1081ff.[68] and in the five lines that conclude the play; they advanced to the front of the stage, spread out in a line and spoke directly to the spectators.

The Newcastle Theatre Company theatre has no fly tower, so an appearance of Medea *ex machina* in a chariot was not possible (nor would it have been desirable in the intimate terms of this production). Instead, we made use of a platform and a costume change to achieve an appropriate effect; Medea appeared upstage right on a platform raised above the playing space, in a golden spotlight and wearing a new gleaming, almost goddess-like gold and black striped dress, a tiara and golden high-heeled sandals; all of this allowed the actress to emphasize her absolute authority over Jason, who stood – and subsequently kneeled – in another blue spotlight upstage centre. There was no other lighting in this scene, so the separation between them was marked.

Finally, no good production of this play is complete without drastic effects for the moments before, during and immediately after the murder of the children. We cross-faded the lights to flood the stage in red during Medea's final speech before going in (beginning at 'Arm yourself, my heart', 1242); and after an intense build-up in the music and in the acting of the Women (half in shadow, half in red light) during the first stanza of Choros 6, we halted the music – an effect designed to shock, as it had never been done in a previous Choros; the stanza during which the sons call out and are then murdered was spoken (and screamed!) unaccompanied. Music only returned, in a sombre and reflective mood, during the 'Ino' stanza that concludes the Choros (1283ff.); and white light was restored only when Jason entered after that for the Finale.

---

[68]This Interlude was declaimed over a percussive accompaniment very different from the music that had accompanied earlier choral odes; and the Women played it as a dialogue in which each spoke one sentence, and the next speaker picked up on the previous one's contribution and developed the idea further. The interaction and the performance gradually became more intense in the lead-up to the final, despairing question.

In all these ways we attempted to make a close translation of Euripides' original *Medea* into an intense and gripping contemporary chamber play for an end-on theatre; and audience opinion was unanimous that we had been highly successful.[69]

3.6.3 Conclusion

Although it is obviously desirable to perform Ancient Greek plays in an outdoor amphitheatre, or an indoor theatre with an arena configuration surrounding the action on three sides, it is a fact that most modern theatres are configured with an end-on audience. I hope that the two case studies, one of comedy and one of tragedy, which I have described above, will have given you some ideas on how a Greek play can successfully be staged in such a space.

3.7 Adieu

Be clear; be faithful to the scripts, but use your imagination; seek out good, accurate and actable translations; and discover the many clues to action provided by the texts. Knowledge of the original circumstances of composition and performance (Chapter 1), of Greek values and beliefs (Chapter 2), and of the formal elements of Greek drama (Chapter 3) should liberate you to explore the true depths of these remarkable plays, and bring the power of the tragedies and the brilliance of the comedies over to modern audiences. I hope that with this book I have helped you to do that. Good luck with your productions and workshops!

---

[69]For more details of how this production of *Medea* was staged cf. the Theatrical Commentary in Ewans 2022: 60–80.

GLOSSARY OF GREEK WORDS

The component parts of the Theatre of Dionysos

Eisodos Side entrance.

Ekkuklēma 'Rolling out machine' – for displaying tableaux from inside the *skēnē*.

Mēchanē The crane used for the appearance from on high of gods, goddesses and demigods.

Orchēstra 'Dance floor' – the playing space.

Skēnē The building where the solo actors changed costumes and masks.

Skēnographia Painted panels on the front wall of the *skēnē*, showing the place that it represents – a palace, a temple, a tent, a cave, open countryside, etc.

Theatron 'Seeing place' – where the audience sat.

Other Greek concepts and objects

Agathos 'Good man' – a person of high social status.

Agōn 'Contest' – a formalized debate.

Aischron Shameful.

Anapaests Choral passages believed to have been 'chanted', halfway between spoken verse and full lyric song.

Aulos The double-reed woodwind instrument, sounding very like an oboe, which accompanied the sung portions of a play.

Chorēgos The sponsor of a production, who paid for the training of the solo actors and choros, and the costumes, props and scenic panels.

Choros The group of actors who played a collective character in tragedy and comedy. They sang and danced their Choroses between, and sometimes short choral interjections inside, dialogue scenes.

Daimōn A god, or a godlike power such as Persuasion, Ruin or Desire.

Dikē Justice – often in the sense of an eye-for-eye revenge.

Kakos 'Bad man', a person of low social status.

Kommos Lyric lamentation shared between a solo actor or actors and choros.

Kyrios The male head of an *oikos*; a woman's father or subsequently her husband, responsible for her.

Miasma Psychic and literal pollution, caused by crime.

Moira Literally, 'lot in life' – the nearest Greek concept to 'destiny'. But it is not predetermined.

Oikos The great household in which a Greek *agathos,* his wife and family, and their slaves lived.

Parabasis Address to the audience by the choros in a comedy.

Phallus Artificial leather penis worn by actors playing male parts in comedy.

Philos Literally 'friend', but primarily referring to a person's relatives and dependents.

Polis A city-state such as Athens, to which all its citizens owed absolute loyalty. Plural *poleis.*

Prosōpon Literally 'face'; the mask worn by actors. Plural *prosōpa.*

Sōphrosynē Modest conduct in a woman, with a heavy emphasis on chastity.

Stichomythia 'Step-speech'; a section in which there is a dialogue conducted in an exchange of individual lines, or pairs of lines, or sometimes half-lines or less.

Thrēnos Lament.

Timē 'Honour'; status, measured in material terms of position and power.

RECOMMENDED READING

Books on the topic

Only four books cover territory directly relevant to this book; all of them are confined to tragedy, and two of them to the actor:

Dunbar, Z. and Harrop, S. (2018), *Greek Tragedy and the Contemporary Actor*, Cham, Switzerland: Palgrave-Macmillan.
   This book begins with two long theoretical chapters explaining why Aristotle and Stanislavski should not be considered as authorities when approaching fifth-century tragedy (I feel that this requires little demonstration). It then settles down to chapters that develop exercises that actors could undertake in preparation for performing Greek tragedy: Acting Sound, Myth, Space and Chorus.

Goldhill, S. (2007), *How to Stage Greek Tragedy Today*, Chicago: Chicago University Press.
   Despite its title, this book unfortunately does not have much to offer to practitioners. The author has never translated or staged a Greek play, so it consists largely of a discussion of productions that he has seen. There are a good many insightful remarks, but the approval of Ted Hughes' 'version' of the *Oresteia* in the translation chapter is problematic, to say the least.

Ley, G. (2014), *Acting Greek Tragedy*, Exeter: University of Exeter Press.
   This book, based on Ley's own workshops in the Exeter Drama Department, investigates, through transactional analysis, the processes needed to stage various kinds of scenes in Greek tragedy. It is sensitive and perceptive. The results are illustrated by video recordings of the workshops, accessible online.

Taplin, O. (1978), *Greek Tragedy in Action,* London: Methuen.
    Although written before the author had practical experience in the rehearsal room, this book provides many insights into the stagecraft of the nine dramas that he analyses.

Further reading

Hughes, A. (2011), *Performing Greek Comedy,* Cambridge: Cambridge University Press.
    This book is devoted to how comedy was performed in the Ancient world. It has an excellent chapter on Ancient acting styles, based on the evidence of vase paintings and figurines.
Ley, G. (2006), *A Short Introduction to the Greek Theater,* 2nd ed. Chicago: Chicago University Press.
    It may be short, but it covers a great deal of ground.
Raeburn, D. (2016), *Greek Tragedies as Plays for Performance*, Hoboken, NJ: Wiley and Sons.
    This book's first chapter is a good introduction to Greek tragedy. However, the analyses of selected plays that follow go into great detail on the intricate metrical patterns of the original Greek verse, which will probably discourage many readers.
Rehm, R. (2016), *Understanding Greek Tragic Theatre,* Abingdon and New York: Routledge.
    A good introductory text with a focus on performance.
Robson, J. (2009), *Aristophanes: An Introduction*, London: Duckworth.
    A good introduction to Aristophanes. It includes a chapter on Theatre Space and Costumes.
Storey, I. and Allan, A. (2013), *A Guide to Ancient Greek Drama* (second edition), Oxford: Blackwell.
    A very good introductory text aimed primarily at Classics students.
Wiles, D. (1997), *Tragedy in Athens: Performance Space and Theatrical Meaning*, Cambridge: Cambridge University Press.
    A good book that delivers exactly what its title suggests – an account of how meaning was shaped in performance in the Athenian theatre.

WORKS CITED

Adkins, A.W.H. (1960), *Merit and Responsibility: A Study in Greek Values*, Oxford: Clarendon Press.

Adkins, A.W.H. (1972), *Moral Values and Political Behaviour in Ancient Greece*, London: Chatto and Windus.

Alexander-Lillicrap, J. (2022), 'Two Escape Tragedies in Translation and Performance: Euripides' *Iphigenia among the Taurians* and *Helen*', PhD thesis, The University of Newcastle, Australia. Available online.

Arnott, P. (1989), *Public and Performance in the Greek Theatre*, London: Routledge.

Arrowsmith W. (1958), 'Introduction to *Orestes*', in D. Greene and R. Lattimore (eds), *Euripides IV: Four Tragedies*, 106–11, Chicago: Chicago University Press.

Bassi, K. (1998), *Acting like Men: Gender, Drama, and Nostalgia in Ancient Greece*, Ann Arbor: Michigan University Press.

Belina, A. and Ewans, M. (2010), 'Taneyev: *Oresteia*', in P. Brown and S. Ograjenšek (eds), *Ancient Drama in Music for the Modern Stage*, 258–84, Oxford: Oxford University Press.

Bierl, A. (2010), 'Die *Orestie* auf der zeitgenössischen postdramatischen Bühne', *Freiburger Universitätsblatter*, 189: 31–74.

Bowie, E. (1988), 'Who is Dikaiopolis?', *The Journal of Hellenic Studies*, 108: 183–5.

Case, S.-E. (1988), *Feminism and Theatre*, Basingstoke: Macmillan.

Compton-Engle, G. (2015), *Costume in the Comedies of Aristophanes*, New York: Cambridge University Press.

Connor, W.R. (1982), 'City Dionysia and Athenian Democracy', *Classica et Mediaevalia*, 40: 7–32.

Dale, A.M. (1969), *Collected Papers*, Cambridge: Cambridge University Press.

Dover, K. (ed.) (1993), *Aristophanes: Frogs*, Oxford: Clarendon Press.

Dunbar, Z. and Harrop, S. (2018), *Greek Tragedy and the Contemporary Actor*, Cham, Switzerland: Palgrave-Macmillan.

Ewans, M. (1975), 'Agamemnon at Aulis: A Study in the *Oresteia*', *Ramus*, 4 (1): 17–32.

Ewans, M. (1980), *Aeschylean Inevitability: A Study of the Oresteia* (Cambridge PhD thesis 1971), University Microfilms: Ann Arbor, Michigan.

Ewans, M. (ed. and trans.) (1995), *Aeschylus: The Oresteia*, London: J.M. Dent.

Ewans, M. (ed. and trans.) (1996a), *Aeschylus: Suppliants and Other Dramas*, London: J.M. Dent.

Ewans, M. (1996b), 'Patterns of Tragedy in Sophocles and Shakespeare', in M. Silk (ed.), *Tragedy and the Tragic*, 438–57, Oxford: Clarendon Press.

Ewans, M. (1999), *Sophocles; Four Dramas of Maturity* (ed. and trans., with G. Ley and G. McCart), London: J.M. Dent.

Ewans, M. (2000), *Sophocles; Three Dramas of Old Age* (ed. and trans., with G. Ley and G. McCart), London: J.M. Dent.

Ewans, M. (ed. and trans.) (2010), *Aristophanes: Lysistrata, The Women's Festival and Frogs*, Norman: Oklahoma University Press.

Ewans, M. (ed. and trans.) (2011), *Aristophanes: Acharnians, Knights, and Peace*, Norman: Oklahoma University Press.

Ewans, M. (ed. and trans.) (2022), *Euripides' Medea: Translation and Theatrical Commentary*, London: Routledge.

Finglass, P. (ed.) (2007), *Sophocles' Electra*, Cambridge: Cambridge University Press.

Goette, H.R. (2007), 'An Archaeological Appendix', in P. Wilson (ed.), *The Greek Theatre and Festivals: Documentary Studies*, 116–21, Oxford: Oxford University Press.

Goldhill, S. (1990), 'The Great Dionysia and Civic Ideology', in Winkler and Zeitlin (eds.), *Nothing to do with Dionysos? Athenian Drama in its Social Context*, 97–129, Princeton: Princeton University Press.

Goldhill, S. (2007), *How to Stage Greek Tragedy Today*, Chicago: Chicago University Press.

Green, J.R. (1994), *Theatre in Ancient Greek Society*, London: Taylor and Francis.

Green, J.R. and Handley, E. (1995), *Images of the Greek Theatre*, London: British Museum Press.

Griffith, M. (ed.) (1999), *Sophocles: Antigone*, Cambridge: Cambridge University Press.

Harrison, T. (1991), *The Trackers of Oxyrhynchus*, London: Faber and Faber.

Heaney, S. (1990), *The Cure at Troy: A Version of Sophocles' Philoctetes*, London: Faber and Faber.

Heaney, S. (2005), *The Burial at Thebes: Sophocles' Antigone*, London: Faber and Faber.

Heinrichs, A. (2012), 'Dionysus' in *The Oxford Classical Dictionary*, Oxford: Oxford University Press.

Henderson, J. (ed.) (1987), *Aristophanes: Lysistrata*, Oxford: Oxford University Press.

Henderson, J. (1991), 'Women and the Athenian Dramatic Festivals', *Transactions of the American Philological Association*, 121: 133–47.

Henderson, J. (ed. and trans.) (1996), *Three Plays by Aristophanes: Staging Women*, New York: Routledge.

Holt, P. (1989), 'The end of the *Trachiniai* and the fate of Herakles', *Journal of Hellenic Studies*, 109: 69–80.

Hughes, A. (2011), *Performing Greek Comedy*, Cambridge: Cambridge University Press.

Hughes, T. (tr.) (1999), *Aeschylus: The Oresteia; A Version*, London: Faber and Faber.

Jones, J. (1962), *On Aristotle and Greek Tragedy*, London: Chatto and Windus.

Kells, J.H. (1973), (ed.) *Sophocles: Electra*, Cambridge: Cambridge University Press.

Kovacs, D. (1987), 'The Way of a God with a Maid in Aeschylus' "Agamemnon"', *Classical Philology*, 82 (4): 326–34.

Lancelyn Green, R. (tr.) (1957), *Two Satyr Plays: Euripides' Cyclops and Sophocles' Ichneutai*, Harmondsworth: Penguin.

Lattimore, R. (tr.) (1951), *The Iliad of Homer*, Chicago: Chicago University Press.

Lebeck, A. (1971), *The "Oresteia": A Study in Language and Structure*, Cambridge MA: Harvard University Press for the Centre for Hellenic Studies.

Lewis, R. (1988), 'An alternative date for Sophocles' *Antigone*', *Greek, Roman and Byzantine Studies*, 29: 35–50.

Ley, G. and Ewans, M. (1985), 'The *Orchestra* as Acting Area in Greek Tragedy', *Ramus*, 14 (2): 75–84.

Ley, G. (1989), 'Agatharchos, Aeschylus, and the Construction of a Skene', *Maia*, N.S., 1 (1): 35–8.

Ley, G. (2006), *A Short Introduction to the Ancient Greek Theater* (second edition), Chicago: Chicago University Press.

Ley, G. (2007), *The Theatricality of Greek Tragedy: Playing Space and Chorus*, Chicago: Chicago University Press.

Ley, G. (2014), *Acting Greek Tragedy*, Exeter: University of Exeter Press.

Liapis, V. and Sidoropoulou, A. (ed.) (2021), *Adapting Greek Tragedy; Contemporary Contexts for Ancient Texts*, Cambridge: Cambridge University Press.

McGuinness, F. (2004), *Euripides' Hecuba: A New Version by Frank McGuiness from a Literal Translation by Fionnualla Murphy*, London: Faber and Faber.

Meineck, P. (2021), 'Forsaking the Fidelity Discourse: The Application of Adaptation' in Liapis and Sidoropoulou 2021, 77ff.

Mitchell, K. (2009), *The Director's Craft: A Handbook for the Theatre*, Abingdon: Routledge.

Mueller, M. (2015), *Objects as Actors: Props and the Poetics of Performance in Greek Tragedy*, Chicago: Chicago University Press.

Neuburg, M. (1992), (trans.) *Aristophanes: Lysistrata*, Arlington Heights: Harlan Davidson.

Olson, S.D. (ed.) (1998), *Aristophanes: Peace*, Oxford: Oxford University Press.

Papastamati-von Mook, C. (2015), 'The Wooden Theatre of Dionysos Eleutherios in Athens: Old Issues, New Research', in Frederiksen, Gebhard and Sokolicek (eds.), *The Architecture of the Ancient Greek Theatre* (Monographs of the Danish Institute at Athens, vol. 17), Aarhus: Aarhus University Press.

Pickard, J. (1893), 'The Relative Position of Actors and Chorus in the Greek Theatre of the Fifth Century BC', *American Journal of Philology*, 14: 68–89, 199–215 and 273–304.

Power, B. (c. 2015), Euripides *Medea: in a Version*, London: Faber and Faber.

Raeburn, D. (2016), *Greek Tragedies as Plays for Performance*, Hoboken, NJ: Wiley and Sons.

Rehm, R. (2002), *The Play of Space: Spatial Transformation in Greek Tragedy*, Princeton: Princeton University Press.

Rudkin, D. (1980), *Euripides:* Hippolytus; *A Version*, London: Heinemann.

Stanford, W.B. (1983), *Greek Tragedy and the Emotions: An Introductory Study*, London: Routledge and Kegan Paul.

Steiner, G. (1975), *After Babel: Aspects of Language and Translation*, Oxford: Oxford University Press.

Steiner, G. (1983), 'Variations sur Créon,' Fondation Hardt, *Entretiens*, 29: 77–96.

Storey, I. and Allan, A. (2013), *A Guide to Ancient Greek Drama* (second edition), Oxford: Blackwell.

Svarlien, D.A. (tr.) (2008), Euripides: *Medea*, Indianapolis: Hackett.

Swift, L. (2010), *The Hidden Chorus: Echoes of Genre in Tragic Lyric*, Oxford: Oxford University Press.

Swift, L. (2016), 'Medea', in L. McClure (ed.), *The Blackwell Companion to Euripides*, Oxford: Blackwell.

Taaffe, L. (1993), *Aristophanes and Women*, London: Routledge.

Taplin, O. (1977), *The Stagecraft of Aeschylus: The Dramatic Use of Exits and Entrances in Greek Tragedy*, Oxford: The Clarendon Press.

Taplin, O. (1978), *Greek Tragedy in Action*, London: Methuen.

Vickers, B. (1973), *Towards Greek Tragedy*, London: Longman.

Wagner, C. (1978), *Diaries Volume I, 1869–1877* (tr. G. Skelton), London: Collins.

Wiles, D. (1997), *Tragedy in Athens: Performance Space and Theatrical Meaning*, Cambridge: Cambridge University Press.

Wiles, D. (2007), *Mask and Performance in Greek Tragedy: from Ancient Festival to Modern Experimentation*, Cambridge: Cambridge University Press.

Wilson, P. (2000), *The Athenian Institution of the Khoregia; The Chorus, the City and the Stage*, Cambridge: Cambridge University Press.

Winnington-Ingram, R.P. (1983), *Studies in Aeschylus*, Cambridge: Cambridge University Press.

Worth, K. (2004), 'Greek Notes in Samuel Beckett's Theatre Art', in E. Hall, F. Macintosh and A. Wrigley (eds.), *Dionysus since 69*, Oxford: Oxford University Press.

Wyles, R. (2011), *Costume in Greek Tragedy*, London: Bloomsbury Academic (Bristol Classical Press).

Zeitlin, F. (1990), 'Playing the Other: Theatre, Theatricality, and the Feminine in Greek Drama', in J. Winkler and F. Zeitlin (eds.), *Nothing to do with Dionysos? Athenian Drama in its Social Context*, 63–9, Princeton: Princeton University Press.

APPENDIX
SOME AUDIO-VISUAL RESOURCES

Except where otherwise stated, these recordings are available on YouTube under the titles given in bold.

A past production cannot be properly assessed unless it has been video recorded; written documentation (programmes, reviews, etc.) and still photographs do not begin to give an idea of what a production was like. So, my survey inevitably omits some important performances. It is a thousand pities, for example, that Diana Rigg's great performance as Medea, and Fiona Shaw's as Medea and as Sophocles' Elektra, were not preserved for posterity. Juliet Stevenson's equally remarkable 1984 BBC TV performance as Antigone is only available in fragments on YouTube (see below).

Michael Cacoyannis' powerful film versions of *Trojan Women, Electra* (Euripides) and *Iphigenia* (at Aulis) have been issued on DVDs.

These assessments are not simply reviews; they are specifically based on the criteria for performance interpretation of Greek drama that have been developed in the main text of this book.

Tragedy

Ancient Greek Theatre Performance: Aeschylus *Agamemnon* – tragedy

Professional
This open-air production by the National Theatre of Greece is undated, and is in modern Greek without subtitles. There is

a very wide end-on playing space with a building behind it, accessed by a ramp from ground level.

The costumes for the Elders (black) and the Messenger (brown) make them look like mediaeval monks, and the choros of ten includes six women – a serious mistake with this play, in which there is an overt and continuous gender conflict between the male Elders and Klytaimestra. They hold long staffs. Movement is very stylized, though there is variety in the delivery of their text – some declaimed in unison, some sung, some spoken by individuals. One of them is marked off by a leather jerkin as the leader, but there is plenty of speech assigned to the others. Literally monotonous drumbeats accompany much of the Choroses, though a stringed instrument is added for Choros 3.

Klytaimestra is costumed in a red dress, with a full-length red robe over it that she discards for the murders. This is over-obvious, especially as Aigisthos appears in red as well. But she is a powerful actress.

Although the other characters are unmasked, Kassandra is played by a man in a white mask with flowing red hair. This completely destroys the power of her crucial scene; the actor presents melodrama instead of true suffering, and self-pity instead of Kassandra's bravery. He tries to milk the emotion of the scene – and fails.

The main general criticism of this production is that characters often face forward, not engaging with the other characters with whom they are in dialogue. This is especially true of the choros in the Messenger, Kassandra and Aigisthos scenes, and it diminishes the emotional impact of the play. And there is far too little movement; in the scene over the bodies (or rather, strangely, only one body, that of Agamemnon), Klytaimestra stands at the top of the ramp, and the Elders are lined up in two rows in the main playing space below; neither moves at all for a scene that positively demands interaction.

Finally, the production is very slow, lasting one hour and forty-three minutes. At times, for example, in the first part of the Kassandra scene, the pacing is so slow that the show almost falls apart. Not recommended.

Ajax by Sophocles directed by Jeff S. Dailey

American Theatre of Actors, n.d.
Professional
This is a sometimes very powerful presentation of one of Sophocles' greatest surviving tragedies, spoilt partially by there being only one camera; some action on the stage takes place just out of its view. But the diction is exemplary throughout. The translation, not credited, is good.

Ajax is set in a square pit surrounded on three sides by blacks, with an upper gallery from which Athena at the beginning of the play, and Odysseus at first in the final scene, speak. All the men from Salamis – Ajax himself, the choros of Sailors, the Messenger and Teucer – strangely wear nothing but a short skirt-like garment, while the generals, Odysseus, Menelaus and Agamemnon, all wear armour and cloaks. Matthew Hanson as Ajax and Madeleine Weber as Tekmessa (beautifully costumed) deliver very physical and passionate portrayals of their roles, as does the Messenger. The Teucer is weaker and fluffs a line towards the end of the play.

There is no music; the Sailors' lines are mostly delivered by individuals, though some are spoken in unison. Movement during the choral odes is minimal. There is no *ekkuklēma*, so we do not see Ajax surrounded by the animals that he has killed; but he is suitably covered in blood. The change of scene to the seashore is effectively handled.

Recommended.

Barnard/Columbia Ancient Drama Group: Euripides' Alcestis (2011)

Student
(Ancient Greek, subtitled)
Actually 2012 according to the credits.
Clare Catenacci's production, performed on a smallish end-on stage, has costumes for the principals inspired by Japanese

ceremonial dress. The choros however are Western – two young men in black who speak, and two young women in black leotards who dance. (This makes nonsense of their line; 'shall I don black clothes?') The servants are also in black. All characters have heavily made-up faces, mostly white with red eye shadow and cheeks, though Death has an imaginative black and white pattern.

Admetus is good, and the music, mostly for piano, flute and guitar, is effective.

This production is ruined for me by the casting of a tall man with very clearly masculine features as Alcestis, who should be quintessentially female. The other eccentricity of casting is Herakles – a young woman with long, purple hair, blue and gold make-up, and a black belt judo costume with a big fur wrap. She enters on a tricycle (with a large toy lion on the handlebars), which she uses later in the play to bring Alcestis back. As her slapstick routines, to the accompaniment of kazoos, are highly effective, this is a less glaring cross-gender casting than that of Alcestis. She also enacts the combat with Death on stage; this is a good idea.

In the final scene, Alcestis only adds a transparent white bridal veil to her costume, so it can easily be seen that the veiled woman is Alcestis. This should not be the case.

Ancient Greek Theatre Performance: Andromache Euripides Loutraki

Professional
(Modern Greek; no subtitles)
This is a highly effective production of an unjustly neglected play. The costumes are 'timeless' – those for the women very successful, those for the men less so. The choros of twelve women both speak and sing, and the lines are divided among them; there is no 'chorus leader'. The dance movements are graceful and expressive. All of the solo actors are good, and the

Andromache is excellent. The only incongruous note is the presence throughout of three old men, seated and holding spears, who take some of the choros lines.

The performance takes place in the open air; a stone-wall building represents the palace. Loutraki, a resort village near Corinth, does not have an ancient theatre, so presumably an open space was supplied with end-on seating for the audience.

Antigóné

Professional

Black and white film shot in Athens in 1961; screenplay and direction by Georges Tzavellas, with Irene Papas as Antigone and Manos Katrakis as Creon. Modern Greek with English subtitles.

This is a classic. The cast includes soldiers and horsemen from the Greek army and 500 extras; Arghyris Kounadis contributes a full-throated orchestral score, and the play is reconceived as a Hollywood-style sword-and-sandals epic. It is remarkably good; the screenplay is an abbreviated version of Sophocles' drama, but omits almost nothing essential; there is a choros, with obviously fake wigs and flowing beards, but still making a major contribution – and their words are spoken by individuals. We see events enacted as they are narrated – including the whirlwind and Antigone's second burial of the corpse, the dissonant birds enveloping Teiresias, and of course the scene in the cave with Haimon's challenge to his father and his suicide. At the end, Creon throws away his crown and walks alone and unarmed out of one of the gates of Thebes – a highly effective final image.

The then young Irene Papas gives a very powerful performance of the title role, and that is matched by Manos Katrakis as Creon. Both Teiresias and the Messenger are also excellent. My only regret is that Antigone's final *kommos* with the choros is heavily abbreviated. You must see this!

Antigone by Sophocles 1984
TV Juliet Stevenson

Antigone by Sophocles episode 1

Professional

Only chunks of about ten minutes each are preserved from this production, which comes from the same team that later presented **Oedipus the King (1986)** – see below. The first chunk is preserved as 'episode 1', and most of the remainder can be viewed consecutively by going to the first link given above. Two episodes are missing after the initial Antigone/Ismene confrontation, so we can only resume watching with the scene where the Soldier (played with English working-class accent and humour) brings the news that someone has buried Polyneikes; and the final moments of Creon's grief are also missing, together with the cast list. Juliet Stevenson is outstanding, indeed mesmerizing as Antigone; but the production has two flaws. First is the excessively free translation by Don Taylor, which aims too hard to be colloquial and contemporary, and in consequence is occasionally banal. Next, is the treatment of the Senators, old men in suits with tails and wearing white cravats, who group into a fixed pattern for each Choros and stand, declaiming either as individuals or in unison. They simply recite, with no movement.

However, the production concept is good; the action takes place in a large hall of which Mussolini would have been proud, with many steps down from huge double doors to the flat playing space, blown-up photographs on the walls of Creon as dictator, and silent soldiers ready to attend to his every whim. The translation leans more than Sophocles' original on 'the power of the State', and Creon himself is played by John Shrapnel in the most dictatorial and tyrannical performance of the role that I have ever seen. In consequence, what we can see of his downfall at the end of the play (clothed in black rather than in the white military-style outfit that he has worn earlier) is the greater.

Antigone (full play)

Amateur

Allen Community College 2015.

This is performed in a small arena stage; there is a *skēnē* behind it with double doors leading down three steps to the main playing area. The translation is by Nicholas Rudall, very actable but also far too free. The actors wear 'classical' dress, and there is a mixed choros (three male, four female), which declaims most of their text, often in a unison that is monotonous and frequently renders the words unintelligible; but there are some solos and some sung verses. They are accompanied by a flute and a drum. The choros' movements are stylized but effective.

Overall, the performance, especially that of the Antigone and Ismene, is far too low-key for the passionate intensity of this tragedy; it is hard to become involved with them. Only in Creon's closing scene with the body of Eurydike (for some strange reason he does not bring in the corpse of Haimon), is there real emotion adequate to the suffering in the text. And he is rather young for the part. The Guard and the (female) Messenger are good. But the great *kommos* before Antigone's final exit is not choreographed, simply spoken – an all too frequent error in productions of this play.

Antigone

Amateur?

2016. Isaac Silva as Creon. Directed by Barbara Hilt.

This is a proscenium arch production. There is no building at the back; simply a dais on which there is a throne. There are fallen columns with graffiti, principally OXI (modern Greek 'NO'), echoing the contemporary protests against the EU's treatment of Greece.

The costumes are 'classical'. An imaginative aspect of the production is that actors behind a scrim mime the suicide by hanging of Jocasta, and the self-blinding of Oedipus during the opening Antigone/Ismene scene; later on the mutual self-destruction of Eteokles and Polyneikes is similarly enacted, and Antigone's burial of Polyneikes. During the Messenger-speech we see and hear Kreon in similar shadow-play, and then Haimon enacting his threat to his father, his clasping of Antigone's corpse and his suicide.

All of this is very effective. Less so is the poor diction (or wrongly placed microphones), which makes much of the rather free prose translation unintelligible; and the almost constant movement of the mixed-sex choros, which pulls focus distractingly from many important solo scenes. They declaim much of their part in unison, also hard to understand; but soloists emerge to speak important lines. The quality of their choroses varies: Choros 3 has very limited movement, Choros 4 has imaginative mime; Choros 6 is performed too slowly to convey its Dionysiac ecstasy.

The Teiresias scene is hammed up, with scenes of modern riots projected on the backdrop.

A serious mistake is made with the *kommos* that precedes Antigone's final exit; there is inappropriate laughter at her from the choros, several times. And the Antigone is not as emotional as her lines require until the very end of the scene. Creon, however, is very compelling in his grief over the two corpses.

Antigone Sophocles

Pro-am?

Directed by Theodora Voutsa in Amsterdam in 2016. She is credited with the English translation and adaptation, but there is also actor improvisation. There are two cameras, and both screens are presented throughout. Modern dress is used.

It is hard to evaluate this production. It is intense, and clearly committed to presenting the play and insisting upon its relevance to contemporary society; but the second of these aims is achieved only at a substantial cost to its success in conveying what Sophocles himself had to say. There is also excessive violence, and a seriously warped interpretation of the role of the choros.

Eleven minutes elapse before Sophocles' opening dialogue between Antigone and Ismene begins. These are filled with mimes anticipating the action, TV newscasts presenting the news from Thebes that the war is over in English and in French, and an incongruous introduction by a Showman. The large choros makes a dynamic appearance. (They are of mixed gender, clad in grey raincoats and boots, and some with hats.) When the play gets under way there are largely individual speakers, with only one or two brief passages in unison. There are improvised scenes in this introduction (one in Dutch); these include the first of several scenes with a 'primordial Antigone' who speaks Greek and encourages the actual Antigone to be strong. Her contributions distract from the drama.

When the Guard has captured Antigone, he hurls her to the ground. He subsequently manhandles her roughly during the 'unwritten laws' speech. Creon does the same during his reply, and first fights her, then rapes her graphically at the end of their *stichomythia*. This is grossly overdone violence. So too at the end of the scene where choros members aggressively separate Antigone and Ismene, and carry them off in separate directions, screaming. This is followed by a really banal improvisation, in which Creon sucks at his mother's breast (!), then proclaims that: 'I am God, your master . . . I Lord, I God.' This extreme megalomania distorts the character and the play.

Predictably, Creon then beats up Haimon. There is too much shouting by both characters in this scene. Before the Eros ode (spoken movingly by one Woman), there is an improvisation about contemporary attacks on women. I can understand the motivation behind this section, but Sophocles' play is at no point concerned with sexual violence (though it does include Kreon's misogyny).

The *kommos* is presented as a trial, with Antigone behind a bar and one of the choros as prosecutor, approved of by the rest of the choros. This reinforces a problem that has been growing earlier; the choros is too hostile to Antigone, and the script of this scene has been altered to enforce this. Sophocles' text at this point certainly includes criticism of the heroine but is nuanced; his Councillors have some sympathy for her plight. At the end Creon forces a long kiss on Antigone; then the choros descends on her in a mob, strips her to her panties and carries her off to her death. Both of these actions are totally inappropriate.

There is another improvised interlude, about 'a girl who dared to be a girl'. Then follows the Teiresias scene; but Creon's denunciations of Teiresias as bribed, and the prophet's consequent anger, are heavily cut. In view of the choros' already exhibited hostility to Antigone, the crucial lines in which they urge Creon to reconsider in light of the prophet's words, and rescue Antigone from her tomb, are also cut. This is a serious omission, since the choros is placed by their verbal and physical support for Creon in this production in a position where their denunciation of him in the Finale is weakened.

This is followed by an improvised address by Antigone (now fully clothed again) to Polyneikes, and then by a further improvisation on feminist themes.

Ismene becomes the Messenger. Eurydike is played by a woman far upstage, draped in white from head to foot, who has had her dialogue cut.

Eurydike's corpse is not brought out. Creon's *apologia* includes words of remorse for killing Antigone, which are significantly not in the original. Ismene takes Creon's crown away from him and speaks the concluding lines.

Caroline Beck as Antigone and Amelie Onzon as Ismene are excellent; but in accordance with the violent production concept, Lolu Ajayhi as Creon is even more overbearing than the part demands.

Bacchae University of Kansas

Student
(Theatre and Film Studies; Katohi, Greece 2006.)
This bilingual production, performed in an Ancient Greek circular amphitheatre, is a disaster. All the male characters are

played by women, except Dionysos – the one male who could well be played by a woman (and has been, successfully, in Gregory McCart's Toowoomba, Queensland production); Pentheus wears a dress, making his transformation under the god's influence, which should be a radical and shocking change from male (military?) garb to female dress, virtually negligible. The choros are in drab colours, and perform uniformly slow, monotonous music (sung, to the accompaniment of a small band) and graceful dances; far away in both sight and sound from the tumultuous ecstasy that Dionysos' exotic Asian bacchantes should manifest. The English translation is shortened (the show runs for only just over an hour), very free and often banal. Agave, dressed in red, brings in Pentheus's golden half-mask rather than a severed head – but she alone has the energy in her dance that the choros should have had. Dionysos in his appearance as a god at the end wrongly wears the same clothes that he did when disguised as the Stranger. Most of what survives of his speech is cut; basically, he just says that mankind is stupid to disobey the gods. Not recommended.

Aeschylus' *Choephoroi* ('Libation Bearers') (2014)

Student

This was a production by the Barnard/Columbia Ancient Drama Group. It was performed in Ancient Greek, with subtitles (which contain some oddities). The performance took place on a proscenium arch stage; the set consisted of some bleachers at the back, and a large mound of sand that represents Agamemnon's grave, and is removed for the second half of the play. There is an attractive original score by Melody Loveless – occasionally too calm and beautiful for the text (especially in Choros 4); and the production is effectively staged in appropriate modern dress. Orestes and Elektra are extremely well performed by Ridge Phelan Monte and Keira Takeshige Boehm. They are both passionate, but wholly without the overacting that plagues many other, much more experienced actors in productions of Greek tragedy.

The only problem with this production is the handling of the choros. They chant or sing, and there is quite a lot of movement, some illustrative, some very graceful. But full composition of a score for a modern performance makes the Choroses, and especially the great *kommos* (in which Orestes and Elektra also both sing), take far too long to perform; they disrupt the tremendous pace at which Aeschylus drives this, one of the most powerful of the surviving tragedies – especially in the second part. It takes 1:38 to perform a play whose running time should be much nearer to sixty-five minutes; and Choros 5, in particular, was set to music that was far too slow. There was even an intermission – placed incorrectly after Choros 3. If there had to be a pause to get rid of the sand, it should have taken place when the scene changes *before* that ode.

Unfortunately, there was a single Chorus Leader conducting all the dialogue of the choros with soloists; this destroyed the chance for interaction between the solo actors and the individuals in the group.

Nonetheless, this is an impressive performance, especially in Elektra's dilemma and subsequent recognition of Orestes, in the climactic scene between Klytaimestra and Orestes, and in the latter's descent into madness in the Finale.

Hecuba by Euripides

Professional?
John McLinn Ross Players, Pine Bluff Arkansas 2016; directed by Cheryl Collins.

An all-black cast in colourful costumes performs a gripping and passionate interpretation of *Hecuba* on a proscenium arch stage, with a large tent back centre. The translation (uncredited) is good but at times free. The choros perform much of their part spoken in unison (there is no music), and this tends to become monotonous; but the vigour of their gestures and movements makes up for this. The murder of the boys and blinding of Polymestor are seen in shadow-play as red light wells up inside the tent for the climax; this is very effective.

Hecuba Pasadena City College

Student

Performing and Communication Arts, directed by Heather Corwin, 2012.

A student production in which inevitably most of the main characters look too young for their parts. But it is a good production with some imaginative touches – for example, the sacrifice of Polyxena is enacted on the raised platform at the rear of the stage, with Neoptolemus and Polyxena speaking their lines in Talthybius' narration. The performance takes place in a small theatre, but it is an arena, with spectators on three sides of the acting area. The costumes are classical. Polyxena is particularly expressive, and there is real excitement at the climax, the emergence of the blinded Polymestor, gloated over by a sadistically joyful group of young women. The translation is free but highly actable.

All of the choros' lines are declaimed in unison, unaccompanied – not only their odes, but also their one- and two-line interventions in the dialogue scenes. Dividing their lines between individuals would have been far more effective. Apart from this the production is a worthy effort.

Εκαβη ΕυριπίδηEuripides Hecuba

Professional

Ancient Elis, 2015. Modern Greek, no subtitles.

This outdoor production is hard to watch. It was shot with only one camera, the lighting for much of the play is very dim so the picture quality is poor, and there is much background noise. In addition, focus is very often pulled by visible actors moving in the background between dressing rooms, behind the tent that is the set. This is distracting.

The choros of six is disappointing; their movements are simple, sometimes just swaying on the spot. But there is a variety of approaches to their text; some declaimed by a spokesperson, some sung to instrumental accompaniment offstage, and one spoken in unison to the accompaniment of clapsticks wielded by the Women themselves. The choros after Agamemnon's departure is effective; the Women kneel, slap their thighs and make solo outcries of grief.

The production as a whole, in 'timeless' costumes, is too stylized (Hecuba emerges after the carnage in the tent with one slightly bloodied hand!); and few of the solo actors rise adequately to the emotions of this powerful tragedy. Odysseus is also far too young.

Euripides HERAKLES: Greek Tragedy with Ancient Music

Student

Barnard Columbia Ancient Drama. Directed by Caleb Stone. New York, 2019. Ancient Greek, no subtitles; 'classical' dress, no masks. In a proscenium arch theatre.

It's not really ancient music, since only small fragments of original scores survive. A composer, Anna Conser, has written music for a reconstruction of the *aulos*, the double oboe-like instrument that accompanied tragedies and comedies in Ancient Greece. The sound is interesting.

This production requires considerable suspension of disbelief. Euripides' choros consists of Old Men, who constantly emphasize their old age and feebleness; here they are played by a group of young women, interspersed with a few young men, all in dresses but wielding long staffs. These staffs are used to great effect in the Choros that celebrates Herakles' achievements.

Amphitryon and Lycus are also played by young women – though in both cases the acting is convincing. Lycus in particular is very good, expressive with both body postures and facial expressions; so too is Megara.

In the Choroses there is usually unison singing, to the accompaniment of the *aulos*, together with some graceful solo dancing. The music is insufficiently varied between the odes, except for the ode of joy when Herakles goes into the palace to kill Lycus, which is very vivid (here all the choros dance) and makes for a great contrast when Iris and Lyssa appear, to the accompaniment of powerful sound effects and red light. Their scene is particularly well acted, with Lyssa's reluctance played against Iris' enjoyment of her task.

In place of an *ekkuklēma*, there is a blackout while the bound Herakles and the bloodstained corpses of Megara and one of the children are preset onstage for the final scene.

Personal interaction is strong throughout – a great contrast with some of the modern Greek productions; and indeed, if you can suspend your disbelief about some of the casting (and follow a translation as you watch), this is a good production of a neglected but powerful play.

Ancient Greek Theatre Performance: Hippolytus Euripides

Professional

This was recorded in the Ancient Greek theatre at Dodoni in 2014, performed by the National Theatre of Greece. The production is in modern Greek without subtitles, but it is a gripping realization of Euripides' tragedy. The costumes are 'timeless' – though Hippolytus and his Huntsmen look like modern Greek shepherds! There is a full orchestral score (pre-recorded) by Dimitri Mitropoulos, in a modern but accessible classical idiom. The choros are in white dresses and head coverings, and their movements are stylized. But there are eleven different speaking actors among them – a welcome relief from productions with one spokesperson. There are no flaws in the casting, with a particularly evil Nurse; though perhaps the actress who plays Phaidra would be more suited to Medea, with her flaming black hair and powerful expressions. The blocking is highly intelligent, and there is none of the overacting that outdoor venues often induce.

'Iphigenia in Tauris' by Euripides performed at HBU

(Houston Baptist University, 2011.)
Student
There are no credits. The translation is clear but free, and heavily cut (the production runs for only just over an hour). The costumes are 'timeless'; long, flowing dresses for the women. A woman seated onstage provides a humming sound almost throughout that distracts from the text. Iphigenia, Orestes and Thoas all overact, at times shouting melodramatically. Contrast the Cowherd and the Messenger/ Pylades, who both have variety of tone and are animated only when necessary.

The main problem with this production is the treatment of the choros. There are only three women, and they stand spread out across the stage in stylized postures and declaim their abbreviated Choroses in unison, unaccompanied. There is no dancing. This becomes very wearisome, since there is no variety; this monotonous mode of delivery is sustained throughout the play.

The temple is imagined as being offstage right, which causes a lack of credibility when Orestes and Pylades arrive on stage and describe its features. The set consists of six columns, four of them surrounding a seat for Iphigenia upstage centre.

Euripides: Medea

and

The original #Medea by #Euripides (*sic*)[1]

Professional

These sites present the same production in 'classical' costume of the Robinson Jeffers adaptation, which is grossly free from the original. There is a monumental set, more like the entrance to a palace than to the home of two exiles; and there is a choros of three, of whom one is the principal speaker. There are no sung or danced Choroses. Under Robert Whitehead's direction, Zoe Caldwell gives a fine interpretation of the title role, which makes one regret that she was not performing an actual translation of *Medea*. Despite the titles under which it has been posted on YouTube, this is not a performance of Euripides' tragedy.

Ancient Greek Theatre Performance: Medea Euripides

Professional

This is a 1998 production from the National Theatre of Greece. It is in modern Greek without subtitles. The running time is over two hours, and although I do not know the language, I am certain that substantial passages of additional text have been inserted into the script.

The production is excessively stylized, but also very melodramatic; there is a lot of shouting, especially from Medea and Jason in their first scene – which leaves Medea with almost

---

[1] This video shows throughout the surtitle 'Hell hath no fury like a woman scorned', and attributes this (mis)quotation from Congreve to Euripides!

nowhere to go in the later scenes where *real* intensity is required. Medea is clothed, far too obviously, in a red dress against the white of the choros and the black of the Nurse and Tutor. The costumes are 'timeless'. The sons are played by faceless, life-sized puppets, removing all empathy from their scenes. Far too much of the play is performed with actors not facing each other when they are supposed to be interacting. Most entries are made through gaps between the curtains that form the backdrop, destroying all sense of the carefully planned spatial geography of Euripides' play. Medea gives a crown of flowers and a veil that she has been wearing in the second scene with Jason to her sons as the presents to the princess; this is ridiculous (why should the poison only work on the princess?). Not recommended.

Medea – National Theatre at home

Professional
This is not on YouTube; you need to subscribe to, or rent from, the National Theatre of Great Britain. It deserves to be seen for the extraordinary performance of the title role by Helen McCrory; but Carrie Cracknell's production is saddled with a 'version' by Ben Power – really an extremely free adaptation – which strays far from Euripides, in most cases unnecessarily so and to the production's detriment. As just one example, much is made of it being set on Jason's new wedding day, which in Euripides has taken place several days before the action begins. It is a great pity that McCrory was not given a more accurate translation of the original tragedy with which to work. Very little is made of the interactions between Medea and the Women of Corinth, which are a key feature in Euripides. And no attempt is made to convey Medea's semi-divine authority in the Finale.

TG (Theatre Group) presents Medea by Euripides

Student

The University of Southampton Theatre Society. No credits.

On an end-on stage, flights of stairs on two sides lead from an upper down to a lower playing space. The translation is free and has a few cuts. Modern dress is used.

This is a very difficult play for a student group to perform. Everyone is naturally too young for their roles – except for the children, who are played implausibly by two young men far too big for the parts. The huge demands of the title role (played by a black actress, the only non-Caucasian in the cast – a good idea in principle) are alleviated by the extraordinary device of having two young men speak some crucial parts of it for her; but she does not have the great emotional range that the role demands. This is especially evident in the scene when Medea is alone with the children, and in the mildness of her tone in the Finale, where she should be imperious and cold. The choros of three young women moves distractingly during Medea's speech about the wretched state of women; and they declaim their Choroses, some parts in unison and some as solos, mostly unaccompanied. There is no choreography; the text is simply recited.

There is intimate, physical contact between Medea and Jason in their first scene together, which seems to me to go against the absolute hostility in the text.

One of the choros mimes the princess in the robe during the Messenger speech, and Creon comes on to clasp the body. Their dumb show is utterly inadequate; if the Messenger had not been placed far away from the audience, he could narrate to full effect the terrifying narrative, which if properly delivered is far more horrific than anything that can be enacted on stage.

The stanza in which the boys call out as they are killed is cut; we simply see a tableau of Medea in red light, sword in hand over the bodies. There are other deviations from Euripides' *mise-en-scène*, and the worst is saved for last;

Medea leaves the bodies of the children with Jason! Not recommended.

Medea – Schauspiel Frankfurt

Professional

Directed by Michael Thalminen in 2013. In German, no subtitles. Performed in modern dress on a large stage with three metallic walls; the rear wall changes to reveal Medea, who spends almost all of the action on a narrow platform around three metres above the stage. This platform is far upstage for most of the play – causing problems for the Medea, who must play her highly emotional scenes at a substantial distance from the audience. Eventually (for the second Jason scene), the rear wall moves forward, and the platform descends to ground level in the final scene, where Medea literally walks over the collapsed Jason.

This is a very spartan production. The cast is reduced to seven, and the children are not seen. But the acting is first-class, and intense – indeed so intense that some scenes simply become shouting matches.

Much of the action takes place surrounded by darkness; the faces and bodies of actors are illuminated by spotlights.

There is no Tutor, as well as no children. The Tutor's lines in his scene with the Nurse are given to a young woman, who stays on to become a choros of one (occasionally joined by the Nurse, who remains on stage after her scene). All the Choroses are spoken, unaccompanied. The only music in the play is during the time when Medea is murdering her sons; music sounds while Choros 6 is replaced by a sequence of projected stylized drawings evoking the stages of life bringing up children.

Medea wears a drab brown coat, which she takes off to reveal a white mini-dress. There are two long, black tears dripping from each of her eyes, and red scratches on her upper chest. When she returns for the Finale, she has changed into a black dress, and cleaned off the marks on her face and body.

In keeping with the production's stylization, Creon faces out into the audience, and at no point makes eye contact with Medea (the same will be true of Jason, and the Messenger). In the encounter with Creon, Constanze Beck, who gives an outstanding, highly emotional and compelling performance as Medea, is aggressive rather than persuasive. She contributes enormous passion to later scenes (sometimes too much so, including when she administers the oath to Aegeus, and in the subsequent speech where she reveals that she will kill her sons); but her final address to the children (delivered to the audience, since there are no children) is rightly quiet and full of pathos.

Jason (Marc-Oliver Schulz) makes his first and second appearances in a blue velvet suit – a very appropriate costume. In the final scene he returns changed into an open-necked shirt and jeans, drenched in water and with his face utterly haggard; his silent acting of his grief when he receives the news that Medea has killed his sons is outstanding.

I understand but do not like this production; it is too stylized, and wholly lacks the realism that is an essential part of Euripides' art. But there is no denying the power of the actors' performances.

THE PLAY BAME Medea

Student
Oxford University BAME Drama Society, 2018. Directed by Francesca Amewudah-Rivers, with Charithra Chandran as Medea.

This is a contemporary adaptation, straying far on many occasions from Euripides' script. It was performed by an enthusiastic and energetic group of Black, Asian and Middle Eastern students, and was greeted with warm applause. But it is unsatisfactory in too many ways. There is a continuous electronic accompaniment to almost all of the dialogue scenes, which is very distracting; and the choroses are set to music, including wordless vocalizes by choros members other than those speaking or singing the text, which make the words almost completely unintelligible. Medea's offstage outcries in Scene 1 and Choros 1 are cut, as is the important passage where Medea tells the Women that she plans to kill her children and they react; and the great monologue to the children before she tells them to go inside is relocated to after the Messenger speech. This is inappropriate and implausible; after the Messenger speech, Medea needs to hasten to kill the children before the Corinthians do.

There are no children, so Medea must tell Jason to go inside to see their bodies. (She has now changed from black to a red top and skirt, and has bloodstained arms.) Her last line is: 'I am no longer afraid'; Euripides' Medea never was. There is a long added choral finale.

Charithra Chandran makes a gallant attempt at the title role and does well with the passages where pathos is needed. But she is not adequate for performing Medea's outbursts of rage and fury.

Medea performance 2018

Student
Warwick University Classics Society
Despite having a student cast who are far too young for the parts, this has a few things going for it; a fairly accurate (uncredited) translation, faithfully followed except for the transposition of the Ino stanza of Choros 6 to the end of the play (Euripides knew better than the director where this stanza should go); a promising set with a staircase to a balcony (though I can't understand why *Medea* is set in a library!); and a large choros (mixed genders, which is a pity) who speak their choroses either in unison or as soloists, some with and some without instrumental accompaniment; there is no dancing. Unfortunately, they are often grouped standing upstage behind the action of scenes, which unavoidably pulls focus. Another, severe problem is that there are no children.

Medea is performed in modern dress, which works well except for Jason; though he does not cut a particularly appealing figure in this play, he is a former hero and attractive to women; he does not deserve to be played as a nerd in a bow tie, braces and spectacles. And the actor, though quite good in his first two scenes with Medea, simply does not have the emotional range for the Finale.

The Medea copes well with the part, given her age; but she cannot summon up the degree of sheer anger that is required.

The decision to mime the deaths of the princess and of Creon during the Messenger speech was misguided; the gruesome scene described in the spoken words is far more powerful than what we see happening upstage behind the speaker.

Apollo Arts production of *Oedipus Rex*

Professional?
Performed in a circular *orchēstra*, this production is in 'timeless' costumes, without masks. Some of the costumes are effective, for example, Oedipus' own; others are much less so – several of the chorus look like mediaeval pages. It is a very clear, and in some of the dialogue scenes, a moving production of a somewhat simplified text (the translator is not mentioned in the credits). The Choroses are declaimed by two spokespersons, one male and the other female, while the other choros members perform rather stylized patterns of movement.

Oedipus the King – Plummer, Welles et al.

Professional
A 1967 film from Universal Studios. Based on the translation by Paul Roche, arguably the best available at that time, and directed by Philip Saville.

This is a very good, highly imaginative cinematic realization of Sophocles' drama with a strong cast. Christopher Plummer plays Oedipus, Orson Welles Teiresias, Lilli Palmer Jocasta and Richard Johnson Creon. Cyril Cusack has a cameo role as the

Messenger from Corinth. All are uniformly excellent. Well worth seeing, although the picture quality of the YouTube posting is not wholly satisfactory.

Oedipus the King (1986)

Professional
Don Taylor directed his actable but very free translation for a BBC studio production of the three Theban plays. *Oedipus the King* is in modern dress, though the choros strangely wear nineteenth-century cravats. The production is imaginative, with a haunting but occasionally banal score by David Bourgeois. Its great strength is that it fields some of the best British acting talent of the 1980s, with stellar casting of the lead roles; Michael Pennington as Oedipus, Claire Bloom as Jocasta, John Shrapnel as Creon and John Gielgud as Teiresias. John Rodney contributes a brilliant cameo as the Corinthian Messenger. Unfortunately, the picture quality of the YouTube posting is not first class.

Sophocles' Oedipus Rex

Student
This 2020 production is by the Warwick Classics Department and Classics Society. There are no credits. The show is bizarre; *Oedipus the Musical* would be a better title, as there is a jazz/ rock score, energetic acting and dancing, and even a group of six go-go girls in red dresses. All the leading actors are miked.

Audience laughter at inappropriate moments shows that the mix of Sophocles' most serious tragedy and this production concept does not work. (There is even song and dance in Teiresias' final, chilling prophecy.)

Oedipus and Jocasta are, inevitably, far too young for the parts, but they act well, especially the Jocasta. The Corinthian Messenger doubles as the Servant who narrates the tragedy inside the house, and he is excellent; the Creon is also good.

Ancient Greek Theatre Performance: Oedipus on Kolonna (*sic*), Sophocles

Professional
Directed by Alexis Minotes, who also played Oedipus.

Modern Greek, no subtitles. 'Timeless' costumes. Performed in an Ancient Greek theatre, which very fortunately for this play happens to have a grove of trees behind it.

Owing to technical difficulties I was only able to watch the first 1:18 of the 1:54 long performance.

There is a large choros with individual speakers and some unison, and also a small amount of song; Choroses and some dialogue are accompanied by pre-recorded instrumental music.

This is a very good production of the play, in the traditional style of modern Greek productions. It is well-cast and well-acted, and the action scenes are vividly conveyed.

Oresteia Agamemnon Part 1 1983 and Part 2 1983

Aeschylus Choephori (*sic*) (Libation Bearers)

Oresteia: Eumenides (The Furies) by Aeschylus

Professional
Peter Hall's controversial 1981 production of the *Oresteia* at the Olivier Theatre on London's Southbank. It is critiqued above in **3.2.1**. I cannot warm to the unnecessary cuts; the all-male masked cast in an indoor space, and in a trilogy where gender conflict is central; the virtuoso but inappropriate quasi-Anglo-Saxon free, alliterative and rhymed translation by Tony Harrison, which is often banal, its compound coinages easily

parodied, and not averse to childish humour ('Shagamemnon'!);[2] the intrusive score by Harrison Birtwistle; and the ritualistic movement, of which there is far too little to bring out the power of these texts. There is little interaction between the characters, and the choros often faces the front from upstage, pulling focus from the solo actors in front of them. Not much is made of the Olivier Theatre's arena shape; large parts of the trilogy are played facing forward, as if in a proscenium arch theatre. Then there is the raised stage, separating some solo actors off from the choros. A colleague of mine once described this *Agamemnon* as a perfect example of Peter Brook's 'deadly theatre', and it is hard for me to disagree with his verdict.

Ancient Greek Theatre Performance – Oresteia Aeschylus

Professional
National Theatre of Greece at Epidaurus, n.d. Directed by Karolos Koun. In modern Greek, no subtitles. The performance takes place on a large square platform, with the windowless brown façade of a building in the background.

This production probably looked more effective live in the huge theatre at Epidaurus than it does on the small screen. White masks are worn, though they do not conceal the mouth. There are intricate patterns of movement and effective groupings for a large chorus, but lots of stylized gestures, and not enough interaction between characters; Orestes, for example, delivers his defence speech in the trial in *Eumenides* out to the central segment of the audience rather than to the jurors (who are widely scattered). And the Priestess does not crawl.

Various means of attack are used to dramatize the choral odes. To take one play; in *Libation Bearers* two Choroses are spoken over an offstage wordless chant, another sung over an

---

[2]Unforgiveable even in the context of *Agamemnon* 1438ff., Klytaimestra's erotically charged denunciation of Agamemnon's infidelity.

instrumental accompaniment, and the *kommos* is declaimed over handheld maracas; later Choroses are spoken over a pulsing string accompaniment, or unaccompanied. The grim final Choros is spoken, effectively, by one Libation Bearer who has taken off her mask.

Given the epic size of the theatre, some effects are disappointing; Agamemnon and Kassandra simply appear seated on a slightly raised platform, rather than in a chariot; Klytaimestra stands at a distance from Agamemnon throughout her scene with him, and does not even face him during the *stichomythia* (but Koun rightly sees that Agamemnon must hesitate before walking on the robes, and Klytaimestra's speech 'There is the sea' is needed to finally persuade him; cf. **3.4.1.4**). She is similarly distant from Kassandra in the next scene.

There is too much reliance on black clothing. Kassandra and the Furies are in black from head to toe (though the prophetess has an orange veil) – both characters invite far more adventurous costuming, since the Libation Bearers are naturally in mourning black (with dark blue veils, matching Elektra's blue dress). Predictably, Klytaimestra and Aigisthos are both clothed in red, with gold trim.

Eumenides is a disappointment. Apollo and Athena, both clad in white with white crowns, speak all their lines from elevated alcoves in the façade – and Apollo even appears again in the Finale. This is a mistake. Apollo is not Athena's equal in this play; his protection is not enough to save Orestes, and his arguments in the trial scene are sophistic; there should be eleven human jurors who vote six to five in favour of the Furies (though Koun wrongly has Athena apparently break a tie between twelve – there is no clear view of the jurors casting their votes). Orestes deserves to be freed, but not vindicated.[3] And Apollo should leave – uniquely, without an exit speech – immediately after the verdict.

There is too little movement in this play – the scene early on between Apollo and the Furies (cf. **1.7**) has no movement from

---

[3]Ewans 1995: 212–14 with bibliography.

either party until the Furies leave late in the scene. But the binding song is very effectively choreographed. However, in the Finale the Furies appear sad rather than angry at the verdict, and with Athena upstage and motionless, a great opportunity for interaction is lost.

The torchlit procession for the exit of the Furies is effective. But they do not receive the crimson cloaks of metics specified in the text (1028), which would have been an important visual symbol of their acceptance into Athens.

Ancient Greek Theatre Performance – Persians, Aeschylus

Professional

Recorded at Epidaurus in 1999. Modern Greek, no subtitles.

This is an interesting, and at many times compelling performance. The set appears at first sight to be strange; a very large number of lights on poles fill the *orchēstra*. But there is an amazing amount of interaction with them, and later in the play the choros pull several of the poles out of the ground and use them as staffs.

The choros is central to this play. They perform most of their part either spoken by individuals or in unison by small groups – and very clearly, unlike in unison in some of the other performances discussed in this Appendix. Later in the play, parts of some Choroses are performed either over wordless melismas or to the accompaniment of an accordion. There are very intricate patterns of movement for the choros; learning and performing these must have been a considerable feat.

The soloists are good, the Messenger being particularly expressive both with his voice and with his body. The costumes include timeless long dresses for Atossa, bronze armour for Dareios, and a long black cloak that Xerxes removes partway through his scene, disclosing a bare chest. The choros wear cream-coloured jackets and robes.

The picture quality is not first-rate, due largely to the amount of the play that is performed in semi-darkness. But it should not put you off watching this performance; two more recent Greek productions of *Persians* (broadcast, but not placed on YouTube) have been far less satisfactory.

Trojan Women Paolo Coruzzi

Professional
Theatro Technis, London 2018. Directed by Paolo Coruzzi.

This was performed on a small end-on stage, littered with newspapers that the Women and Hecuba hurl around at the end in red light to symbolize the destruction of Troy. The three women of the choros wear black robes with hoods, and white half-masks. They speak their lines in unison, and there is some movement, with musical accompaniment.

It is not clear why the choros is costumed like this, since the principal actors wear modern dress. Their performance is of high quality, but either the microphone is misplaced or the diction of some of the actresses is poor – quite a lot of the translation is hard to understand. Despite this problem, Demi Pappa as Andromache gives a powerful performance of her character's grief; Camille Krieg as Kassandra is also good, though insufficiently crazed. And Susan Kempster as Hecuba navigates the part's shifting moods, and its transitions from high emotion to dialectic, very well.

Comedy

Ancient Greek Theatre Performance: Acharnians, Aristophanes, Delphi

Professional
It was actually performed at Epidaurus in 2005. Modern Greek, no subtitles.

This is an excellent production of one of Aristophanes' best plays. It is very physically active and full of stage business, some of it extending the text, for example, in the Bridesmaid scene. Costumes are a mixture of ancient, for the Ambassadors and the soldiers, including Lamachos, and modern for most of the other characters.

The choros plays a substantial part in this comedy. They speak some lines, but sing in unison all that was sung in the original over a pre-recorded soundtrack of modern Greek music; there are complex movements, and there is no one spokesperson; all contribute equally to the dialogue.

I don't understand why Euripides wears a long, quasi-classical robe rather than his beggar's costume; the Megarian acts very well in his slapstick interaction with Dikaiopolis, but has the wrong physique for the role – his build is far too ample to play a victim of dire starvation; and for some strange reason the Boiotian takes away with him the birds that he was supposed to be selling to Dikaiopolis in exchange for the Informer. Otherwise, my only criticism is of the coy modern Greek habit of having young women who are sex objects played by men – in this play the Megarian's daughters and the Two Sexy Girls in the Finale, who don't look sexy at all.

Lakis Lazopoulos as Dikaiopolis sustains his very long role with an outstanding performance, and the audience showed great enthusiasm both during the show and at the end. Recommended.

The Birds by Aristophanes

Student
Georgia Southern Entertainment
A student production in Wyoming, directed by Lisa L. Abbott

This is an energetic and very entertaining production. It is in modern dress, and uses a fairly good translation (if you don't mind rhyming verse). There is lots of slapstick, most of it justified by the text. The choros numbers five, and their choreography is effective. They declaim much of their text in unison, but the words are generally clear.

There are some deviations from Aristophanes; Euelpides takes part in the second half of the play, and there are some interpolated jokes (mostly metatheatrical). Pisthetairos' crude sexual threats to Iris are cut; but he clearly fancies her, and he asks for and gets her instead of Basileia as his consort in the closing scene. The play ends, as it should, with a dance celebrating the wedding. Worth watching.

The Clouds by Aristophanes

Amateur
Bergen Community College. Directed by Ken Bonnafons.
A 'classical' dress production on a stage with many levels, in a proscenium arch theatre.
This is an imaginative production of *Clouds*, which is arguably the hardest Aristophanic comedy to bring over to a modern audience. Some of the comic sequences seem laboured, but other scenes – especially the contest between the Right and Wrong Arguments – work well. The Clouds are represented by three women in silver – two in minidresses and one in a pantsuit – occasionally alternated by three other speakers wearing standard 'classical' costumes.

The Clouds by Aristophanes (Theatre Performance)

Student
Bard College Berlin. A cast of international students directed by Maria Khan, in an abbreviated version (under fifty-five minutes), but one which includes all the essential scenes.
This hardly counts as a theatre performance, as it takes place in a dilapidated room and has no set; the cast just wear everyday contemporary clothes. There is no music and very few props; Socrates is played by a woman wearing a huge black beard, and the Clouds are two young women in white half-masks, who undulate continuously. The two Arguments

are a very modestly dressed young woman up against one in a sexy dress; their scene is effective. But, in general, the standard of the acting is not very good.

Aristophanes' Frogs

Student
Warwick University Classics Society 2019 directed by Kelsi Russell.
A valiant student attempt at a difficult play. There are imaginative ideas in the production, but there is insufficient pace, and the classics students mostly lack the precise sense of comic timing that is needed for Aristophanes. Several parts of the play, including the whole *parabasis* and the dialogue between Xanthias and his fellow-slave, become fully sung musical numbers. In the contest between the two poets, the section in which they parody each other's prologues, lyrics and monodies is entirely cut.

Aristophanes Frogs (The Cambridge Greek Play, 2013)

Professional
Directed by Helen Eastman. Ancient Greek with subtitles.
This is a vividly inventive production, owing much to vaudeville and slapstick. There is a brass band onstage, and a chorus who sing 'Brekekex koax koax' (which reappears as the Finale) as a full musical number. There are interpolations, and in the subtitles both deliberate mistranslations and many jokes that use contemporary references; and there is free interpolation of *lazzi* in the stage action. The *parabasis*, the lyric section of the poetry contest and the political debate that leads to Dionysos' final decision, are all cut (thus omitting the two key messages of Aristophanes' play). But nothing so serious is allowed to interrupt the riotous humour of this performance, in which the 'Throne of Tragedy' is a toilet. Eastman goes

against almost everything that I have argued for in this book – but she undoubtedly succeeds in her own aim, which is clearly to give the audience a good time at all costs, including that of any fidelity to Aristophanes' original comic creation.

Aristophanes Frogs by Matthew McCann (2013)

Pro-am?

This is a very free, and not very good, British musical adaptation. It is performed in 'classical' dress, but modern jokes, contemporary references (now outdated) and other materials are freely interpolated, including a superfluous song for Dionysos about the difficulty of making a choice between the two poets. The *parabasis* is replaced by a Q & A session with the audience, and the scene between Xanthias and the Old Slave is replaced by a passé Hollywood actress lamenting her decline. The contest between the poets is simplified, and the parodies of lyrics and monodies are omitted (admittedly these are very difficult to make effective for a modern audience).

Acschylus and Euripides shout at each other with little variation of tone (the Dionysos also lacks the necessary expressive range for the part). At the end, the victorious Aeschylus delivers a homily to the audience on our need to preserve our planet, Gaia – an extremely worthy sentiment, but one which seems to be arbitrarily tacked on to what is left in this version of Aristophanes' play. Not recommended.

Aristophanes Lysistrata (2004)

Student

Loyola University New Orleans, directed by Donald Brady.

A vigorous and energetic production, in which, however, the Choroses are replaced by sung, heavily accompanied choruses in the style of a modern musical, with new lyrics.

Apart from these, the translation, though occasionally free, is racy and vivid. However, it bowdlerizes the original in the scene between Kinesias and the Spartan Herald, and in the working out of the peace treaty on the body of Reconciliation. Also, Lysistrata offers in the Finale that the women will give the men 'provisions' rather than 'what is in our boxes' – strange, as both the text and the accompanying action elsewhere in the production are rightly full of the original's sexual innuendo.

The chorus of men wear military uniform that is Roman rather than Greek, and the women wear 'timeless', flowing dresses – except for Lysistrata, who is in a modern blouse and pants (which contrasts oddly in the *agōn* with the classical *chiton* of the 'Secretary of State for Defence'), and Lampito, who is costumed as a Wagnerian Valkyrie complete with winged helmet. The males wield splendid phalluses, which are quite rightly erect in the later parts of the play.

My main objection to this otherwise fine production is that the choruses are portrayed as young men and women. My own 2005 production proved that students can quite easily play the parts of Old Men and Old Women, and in my view this is essential to the play.

However, this performance received a standing ovation, which in many respects was thoroughly deserved.

Lysistrata full play – Baruch College: Baruch Performing Arts Center

Student

A vigorous, exciting, sexy but occasionally overwrought production, with much (mostly justifiable) slapstick and a slightly free but effective translation. The choroses, for three Old Women and three Old Men, are declaimed unaccompanied. Dress is a mixture of ancient and modern. The closing scene of reconciliation is rather flat, but redeemed by the following, final song and dance number. Recommended.

NYRF 2008 – Lysistrata

Festival

New York Renaissance Faire, adapted and directed by Lionel Ruland.

This is an outdoor production in 'classical' dress. The rhyming translation is slightly off-putting, as are the silent 'e 's at the end of proper names. But, it is a spirited, vigorous production, with plenty of sexual innuendo in the body movements, even though the text is a little bowdlerized. Economies of scale meant that the Old Women were played by members of the original gathering of young women. The choros members of both sexes strip to body stockings with fig leaves in the central Choros, but strangely, Reconciliation wears a T-shirt and shorts. This production is good fun, and captures much of the spirit of the play.

Lysistrata

Amateur?

Lone Brick Theatre Company 2014.

This is an unsatisfactory production. The play is spiced up with numerous danced interludes for the male and female choruses, mainly to jazz or soul music; and there are many blackouts between scenes (there should be none). The effect of both is to destroy the momentum of a play that originally built steadily to and beyond its climax. *Lysistrata* should run for less than eighty minutes; because of the additions, this version runs for ninety-five.

Then there is the problem of the translation, which is euphemistic and contains none of Aristophanes' original four-letter words (e.g. LYSISTRATA: 'To put it bluntly, *we are crazy to get laid*'; Aristophanes actually did put it bluntly!). This of all comedies demands explicit sexual language. The version (uncredited) is also very free, especially in the Commissioner's opening speech and his *agōn* with Lysistrata.

The players are all young, except for the leader of the Choros of Old Women, who is grey-haired. The rest of the chorus make no attempt to act as Old Men and Women; indeed, the young women of the female chorus wear sexually revealing outfits – mostly corsets and stockings – (as do Kalonike and Myrrhine, with more justification); and in one interlude they do bumps and grinds over the bodies of the male chorus members.

Lysistrata

Student
Warwick University Classics Society 2016. New (sometimes free) translation by Clive Letchford.

A bare, wide end-on stage with a lit archway for the entry to the Acropolis. This was a production by classics students, and the women in particular exhibited energy; but, naturally, the actors lacked a professional sense of comic timing. No attempt was made to portray the choros members as Old Men and Old Women, though we found in my first Newcastle production that students can easily do this. There was a lot of cross-gender casting; the male choros included two girls, and the Executive was also played by a woman; Reconciliation was a drag queen. All of this is highly undesirable in a play whose whole theme is female/male conflict! Choroses were delivered unaccompanied, partly by solo actors and partly in unison.

For some strange reason, Kinesias and the Spartan Herald sported giant phalluses, but the Ambassadors' erections were concealed in their trousers. The very funny scene of the four would-be escapees from the citadel was omitted, and Lampito simply declaimed the final song over instrumental music.

Warwick University Classics Performance of Aristophanes' Thesmophoriazusai 2015

Student
This is not a satisfactory production, even by student standards (though it was enthusiastically received by the

audience). The set consisted simply of blacks on three sides, five chairs for the choros, an altar and a low table, on which the speakers stood during the festival meeting. Euripides was played by a woman; Kleisthenes was neither in drag nor openly gay; the In-Law was not stripped naked, as the script requires, when his gender is discovered; and Euripides was not in disguise when he appeared as Menelaos. There was quite rightly plenty of crude humour, but many opportunities for comic effect provided by Aristophanes were missed. There was no *parabasis*, and the choreography was very limited (the circular dance in Choros 5 was not circular at all!). For no good reason the girl playing Fawn was unwilling, and Euripides as the Old Woman dragged her around by the hair. She did not perform a seductive dance, nor sit on the Policeman's lap. And the In-Law's virtuoso 'Andromeda' monody, a highlight of the play, was abbreviated almost to nothing.

* * *

Links to my own first nine (student) productions may be found at https://uoncc.wordpress.com/2014/03/20/ewansarchive/.

The picture quality is not very good for the three *Oresteia* plays, because of the limited video cameras available to us in the early 1980s. The best production, and the best recording, is *Antigone*. (There is an interview with me after the closing credits.)

My professional production of *Medea* in a smallish theatre with an end-on audience may be found on YouTube at https://youtu.be/B5No7E56zxE or by entering Euripides Medea Newcastle Australia 2021. It is a recording of the dress rehearsal, and a few errors were made that were corrected the following night for the opening.

My professional production of *Lysistrata* may be found on YouTube by entering Aristophanes Lysistrata Newcastle NSW 2022. This also is a recording of the dress rehearsal.

INDEX